31

for Stephen & Ha

Poetry's
Geographies

stephen

Lowh

4/4/23

for srephan

with besr wishes

Poetry's Geographies

A Transatlantic Anthology of Translations

Edited by
Katherine M. Hedeen
& Zoë Skoulding

Shearsman Books

First published in the United Kingdom in 2022 by
Shearsman Books
P O Box 4239
Swindon
SN3 9FN

Shearsman Books Ltd Registered Office
30–31 St. James Place, Mangotsfield, Bristol BS16 9JB
(this address not for correspondence)

www.shearsman.com

ISBN 978-1-84861-851-0

Co-published simultaneously in the U.S.A. by Eulalia Books, Latrobe, PA.

Cover art: Román Antopolsky

Contents

Stephen Watts

Introduction

Zoë Skoulding

The abrupt halt to travel brought about by the pandemic in 2020 coincided with the initial stages of gathering work for this anthology. With readings and poetry festivals cancelled, postponed or shifted into the cold blue light of Zoom, the network of human connections that sustain poetry as a living, embodied form looked suddenly precarious. At the same time, translating and reading poetry in translation had never seemed more urgent. As the world shrank to the scale of a confined domestic space, poetry translation was a chance to live in the multiplicity of languages and the spaces of relation that it opens up. It was not just the pandemic that presented this urgency to us as editors, but the previous four years in our respective countries of the USA and the UK. The election of Trump and the UK's Brexit vote paralleled each other as a turn towards isolationist politics and also towards the isolation of anglophone cultures from their multilingual surroundings.

Our belief that poetry could in some way address this situation was informed by a particular experience of poetry in social spaces, especially the spaces of European and Latin American international poetry festivals that regularly bring poets together to read in different languages with translation, and it was in such an event in Buenos Aires in 2018 that the idea for this anthology came about. The sense of an energetic, outward-looking poetry community spanning different Latin American countries, full of lively frictions and profound friendships, might be seen as contrasting with what is often a more insular experience of poetry in the UK and USA, where translation tends to be less valued and less visible as a regular aspect of literary culture. Nevertheless, even in the Anglosphere, translation is a mode of relation that connects poetry and poets in multiple and often unanticipated ways. Operating outside the larger-scale commercial interests of fiction in translation, it is both a form of reading and a means of sustaining conversations across cultures. We have aimed in this anthology to bring the work of translation, including our own, into focus. The translators include Forrest Gander, Don Mee Choi, Johannes Göransson, Erín Moure, Kareem James Abu-Zeid, Sasha Dugdale, Ghazal Mosadeq, Dan Eltringham, Stephen

Watts and Meena Kandasamy, while the poets translated are from Mexico, Korea, Galicia, Palestine, Russia, Sweden, Iran, Guatemala, Cuba, India and France – and this list in itself poses certain profound questions about maps and their implications. For this reason, we decided against foregrounding national identifications in the headings of each contribution, but the poems, commentaries and biographical notes, read together, form glimpses of a world that does not appear on any map. Most translators chose living poets; two did not. Our desire to include a range of source languages, as well as the practical constraints of making an anthology, meant that we could not ask many translators we admire, while the backdrop of the pandemic, with its uneven pressures, meant that not everyone we asked was able to participate. In this limited selection, we have deliberately resisted providing an overview of contemporary poetry translation: these are examples of crossed paths rather than a map, because this is how we understand the movement of poetry across languages in translational cartographies that intersect, but do not wholly coincide, with geopolitical circumstances.

In inviting contributors to write about the practice of translation, we were inspired by Robert Sheppard and James Byrne's *Atlantic Drift: An Anthology of Poetry and Poetics* (Arc, 2017), which, although it is not concerned with translation, usefully places poetics as well as poetry in dialogue. Sophie Collins's innovative investigation into multiple forms of translation, including the intralingual and intersemiotic, *Currently & Emotion: Translations* (Test Centre, 2016), is another valuable precursor that disturbs linguistic boundaries and the hierarchy of source text and translation. Our selection follows lines between translators and the poets they translate as a means of enquiring into the spaces and practices that emerge through the act of translation. These lines do not necessarily cross the Atlantic, but the premise of the anthology was that the translators should be from (or based) either side of the Atlantic Ocean. We invited poet-translators from North America and the UK to choose poets to translate into English, resulting in a deliberately unruly poetic geography. Far from the smooth loops and starry clusters of international flight paths, the haphazard map made by these poets emerges erratically from chance encounters, personal synergies, political commitments and tangles of literary influence. Maps are inherently untruthful, as everyone knows: the idea of "world" is unevenly distributed, as is an idea like the "transatlantic", with its overtones of trade routes, military treaties and a violent history of slavery. Maps represent and make visible, as do anthologies, but in offering the quickest route from A to B they also – inevitably – conceal and distort. The present collection is offered in a more psychogeographical vein as a form of countermapping.

Rather than making the world more transparent and "accessible" for quick consumption, poetry and its translation can sustain *opacité*, in the sense described by Édouard Glissant, as an opaqueness that allows the Other to exist in full, not to be reduced or subordinated.[1] In his understanding of relation as fundamental to the Americas, he presents a model for global community in which cultures are not assimilated into dominant paradigms but retain their capacity for multiplicity, difference and resistance. "Errantry", another of Glissant's key terms, describes the process of navigating the plurality of cultural experience.[2] Rather than representing a nation, culture or language by reflecting it as an apparent whole, or from an exterior viewpoint, poetry translation creates patterns of interference through transformative, situated encounter. Errantry, with its connection to error as well as wandering, is at the heart of every act of translation, since the translated text is never a mirror of its source but a diffraction – and diffraction, too, is part of Glissant's vocabulary of poetic relation. How can we understand poetry's movement in and through the worlds it creates? Birgit Mara Kaiser connects Glissant's thinking with that of the theoretical physicist Karen Barad in order to address the difficulties of the term "world literature" – a term that too often perpetuates static and reductive hierarchies, or as Emily Apter warns, creates a market-driven illusion of universal accessibility.[3] For Barad, diffraction is understood in the context of quantum physics as both a behaviour of matter and a means of observing it, since the behaviour of matter changes according to the way in which it is observed. Barad argues that Newtonian physics and Cartesian epistemology are alike up-ended by the realization that the world is not reducible to the atom as a basic building block. Kaiser

---

[1] Édouard Glissant, *Poetics of Relation*, trans. Betsy Wing (Ann Arbor, MI: University of Michigan Press, 1997), 191.

[2] Glissant, 11.

[3] Emily Apter, *Against World Literature: On the Politics of Untranslatability* (London and New York: Verso, 2013).

draws specifically on Barad's neologism *spacetimemattering* to describe the process at work in reading across cultures, drawing attention to the following passage of Barad's:

> The world is a dynamic process of intra-activity in the ongoing reconfiguring of locally determinate causal structures with determinate boundaries, properties, meanings, and patterns of marks on bodies. This ongoing flow of agency through which "part" of the world makes itself differentially intelligible to another "part" of the world and through which local causal structures, boundaries, and properties are stabilized and destabilized does not take place in space and time but in the making of spacetime itself. The world is an ongoing open process of mattering through which "mattering" itself acquires meaning and form in the realization of different agential possibilities.[4]

From this understanding, Kaiser observes: "It is this focus on the differential emergence of entities in intra-action that greatly challenges our habits of thought, used to conceiving of bodies etc. as separate, individual (atomistic) entities *in* the world."[5] What is at stake is nothing less than a remaking of what we mean by "world", which can no longer be seen as a stable backdrop to the encounters that take place within it, but which is instead formed and reformed by them, continuously. These cultural extrapolations from quantum thought offer a way of reading and writing across cultures that emphasizes dynamic change and involvement, troubling borders of all kinds.

Relations between poet and translator are also subject to the destabilizing of boundaries and properties, since poets are frequently also translators, educators, critics, publishers and organizers of events, their practice informed by these activities as well as by reading, collaborating and performing in international contexts. They are engaged in a process that Barad describes as "making worlds", that is: "making specific worldly configurations – not in the sense of making them up *ex nihilo*, or out

---

[4] Karen Barad, "Posthumanist Performativity: Toward an Understanding of How Matter Comes to Matter." *Signs* 28, no. 3 (2003): 801–31, 817.

[5] Birgit Mara Kaiser, "Worlding CompLit: Diffractive Reading with Barad, Glissant and Nancy," *Parallax* 20, no. 3 (2014): 274–287, 278.

of language, beliefs, or ideas, but in the sense of materially engaging as part of the world in giving it specific material form."[6] Nation may be contextual, strategic, or reconfigured in translation viewed as a decolonial practice, while languages and cultures intra-act, diffracted by the poem. Kareem James Abu-Zeid reflects on his own Egyptian-American identity and that of the Palestinian poet Najwan Darwish, noting that both translator and poet inhabit these terms but are strongly anti-nationalist, and that the poems "cross between Europe and Asia, and between the Turkish language and the Arabic one before making a further crossing: the Transatlantic one, into (a mostly American mode of) English." These oceanic movements are not accidental, but deliberate consequences of a form that enables and encourages the fluid connections of language: "It is, perhaps, no coincidence that the Arabic word *bahr* means both 'poetic meter' and 'sea'. When we are creating and translating poetry, we are sailing the sea, perhaps many seas, and bringing seemingly disparate realities together."

We wanted to create a frame for encountering translation that does not bracket off poetry within national determinations that it may resist or evade, but that describes some of its movements and relations through the practice of translating. This is a process that is notoriously difficult to capture, yet it is crucial if we are to counter some misapprehensions that often accompany the word "translation". As Michael Cronin observes:

> The notion of carrying across words or ideas from location to location would appear to lie easily with the etymological promise in the anglophone world of trans-latio, across-carry-ing. Indeed, it is arguably the perception of translation as a form of transport that leads to a particular logic of inversion where the translation product is privileged over the translation process. The focus is on destination. How the translation gets there or what happens on the way is of no particular interest. The basic nature of the message, like the travellers seated in the jet plane, should remain unchanged.[7]

[6] Karen Barad, *Meeting the Universe Halfway: Quantum Physics and the Entanglement of Matter and Meaning* (Durham: Duke University Press), 91.

[7] Michael Cronin, *Eco-Translation: Translation and Ecology in the Age of the Anthropocene* (Abingdon and New York: Routledge, 2017), 63.

The form of the translator's note, developed here into statements of translation poetics, allows for a closer view of "what happens on the way", which is a very particular interest of this anthology. The tendency to regard English as a vehicle sustains an illusion of fluid global connectedness that masks difference and inequality, while the process of translating a poem makes visible the friction between languages. The poetics of translation bring into view the role of the "poet-translator", although this is not a straightforward term. It suggests that the role of translator is secondary or additional to that of being a poet and so, it creates a confusion that contributes to the diminishing of translation as an art form. If a poet is someone who writes poetry, then surely a translator, who must create the poem in the receiving language, is also a poet. Yet at the same time, it is worth observing that in many other languages, it is far more ordinary for poets to regard translation as part of the work of being a poet than it is in English. Beyond the influence of the creative writing workshop, with its distinctly anglophone pedagogies, generations of poets have learned to write by translating, so one could say that the poet-translator is a translator first, and only then a poet.

In the background is a set of problematic assumptions related to the English language, including the idea of the "special relationship" between the UK and USA. The nexus of global power that created the dominance of English has waned, but its hegemonic reach remains, and is bound up with the international circulation of poetry. Johannes Göransson argues that poetry translation exposes closely protected values, for example the belief in the expression of interiority in US poetry that became part of the promotion of a hegemonic global culture. Yet translation can also enable "transgressive circulation" that embraces the excluded "foreign body". This is important, he writes, because "a poetry that is profoundly engaged with foreign poetry is a poetry that is aware that nations are not homogeneous, that while the institutions of literature are almost always hierarchical, writing itself is not."[8] In creating this anthology, our belief is that translators, and particularly translators of poetry, have the potential to mediate English, creating what Göransson and Joyelle McSweeney have described as a

---

[8] Johannes Göransson, *Transgressive Circulation: Essays on Translation* (Blacksburg, VA: Noemi Press, 2018), 90.

"deformation zone" that can critique its effects,[9] and which can also form connections that stretch across languages and continents. Rather than mirroring in another language, translation diffracts, creating far-reaching ripple effects.

The double role of the poet-translator intensifies this intra-action. Korean-American poet Don Mee Choi's translations of the Korean poet Kim Hyesoon are illuminated by Choi's own most recent work, not itself a translation although it uses many translation techniques, the award-winning *DMZ Colony* (Seattle, WA: Wave Books, 2020). Its title draws attention to the irony of what is called the "demilitarized zone" of the Korean border that is in fact one of the most militarized borders in the world. The continuing US military presence in South Korea, a neocolonial overlay of state power, lies behind the dissonance between places, languages and sensory impressions that shadows Choi's immigrant perspective in the US. She describes the radically displaced position of the translator, who must adopt translation an "anti-neocolonial mode":

> South Korea has been a neocolony of the US since 1945. So, in brief, this is the linguistic context of my translation process. It is not joyfully cross-cultural. It impacts what I choose to translate and how I translate it. For me, contextualizing the work may be the most important part of my translation process…. My translation intent has nothing to do with personal growth, intellectual exercise, or cultural exchange, which implies an equal standing of some sort. South Korea and the U.S. are not equal. I am not transnationally equal. My intent is to expose what a neocolony is, what it does to its own, what it eats and shits. Kim Hyesoon's poetry reveals all this, and this is why I translate her work.[10]

In her essay for this volume, Choi locates South Korea's place in a

---

[9] Johannes Göransson and Joyelle McSweeney, *Deformation Zone: On Translation* (New York: Ugly Duckling Presse, 2012).

[10] Don Mee Choi, "Translation in Process: From 'I'm OK, I'm Pig,'" *Lantern Review*, Issue 6, http://lanternreview.com/issue6/DonMeeChoi_TranslationinProcess.html Accessed 28 August 2022.

continuation of the Cold War that has never ended on the peninsula. Such a territory bristling with military bases, she explains, is known in military terminology as a "Lily Pad." It is in this context, rather than from any botanical reference that she derives her "lilymethod" of translating Kim Hyesoon's "IS THERE WHITE LIGHT FOR US?",[11] in which the conjoined word 백합질식사시키는, literally "lilyasphyxiationmake," is translated as as "lilyasphyxiating," then revised to "lilyphyxiating." She writes: "I removed the kidney-resembling *a*. Such precise removal requires what translators like to call skill. I prefer to call it lilymethod." The surgical irony of this statement draws attention to the translation's friction against English, making the "foreign body" of the translated text, in Göransson's terms, powerfully felt. If the US military presence in South Korea can be described as an innocuous flower, so too can the pressure placed on English by Choi's nuanced translation.

The lily makes an appearance, too, in Canadian poet Erín Moure's translation of Galician poet Chus Pato, which likewise comes from a translating relationship of many years that has inflected Moure's own writing. "Stalker" sets off from the Tarkovsky film, with its journey to the Zone of what is most desired, but becomes an investigation made through language, zigzagging through alphabets and images. Moure insists that Pato is not a hermetic writer but a materialist one; the path through through language is a path between experiences of the world, organized through the alphabet. The list begins with anthracite, hard coal, metamorphic rock. It proceeds through belladonna, carbuncle, digitalis, foxglove, the geological and botanical linked to the body, *gorxa* translated as gorget, a necklace, metal ornament. The alphabet has its own materiality, drawing the world into a particular order through the Galician language. N is for *nenufar* in Pato's poem, which Moure translates by an explicatory sleight of hand, via Latin as "nymphaeaceae." But this is in the vein of the poem, which leads to Monet, to Paris, the Jeu de Paume and a pediment marking French state control of Basque regions. Monet's waterlily becomes the lost waterlily of the Antela lake in the Ourense region of Galicia, drained by Franco to catastrophic environmental effect. The Limia or Lima River, fed by the lake was

---

[11] Kim Hyesoon, *Nalgae hwansangt'ong* [*Phantom Pain Wings*], (Seoul: Munhakkwajisŏngsa, 2019), 162.

identified by Romans as Lethe, the river of forgetting. The waterlily that floats as a referent glimpsed in memory is made visible through the diffractions of the poem: it does not settle into an emblem of original Galician identity. There is no way to read this poem without following language structures into an understanding of Galicia's suppression and exploitation by the Spanish state, but the poem is also a journey into the Zone of bifurcating paths. The lost Timurid empire is evoked through the five part structure of the poem, a pentalogy, echoing the *Kamsa of Nezāmi*, the quintet of narrative poems written in its capital Herat, an oasis city in a fertile river valley now desolate under the Taliban. Moure writes: "These heightened issues of positionality accompany my every translational move, especially in English, language of absorptive capital." Moure, as an anglophone poet in Montréal, finds in Pato a way to locate her own multilingual poetics that makes English permeable to other languages: "What if national determinations in a unitary state (España Canadá) created more borderlands, thus more potential for overlap, irruption, thus freedoms!"[12]

Ghazal Mosadeq's practice as a poet and editor of Pamenar Press has focused on experimental techniques as a means of thinking cross-culturally. Here, her chosen poet is Mehdi Akhavan Saless (1928–1990, Mashad, Iran), published under the pseudonym M. Omid. His work is often concerned with the Iranian coup of 1953, the removal of a democratically elected government by the UK and USA in an attempt to maintain power over oil supplies, which continues to have an impact in contemporary Iran, the Middle East and beyond. In this allegorical poetry, the coded message is expected. Mosadeq explains that "Persian literature has survived many oppressive regimes over centuries by habitually obscuring its meaning." It has, in this sense, the opacity described by Glissant, so the translator must navigate this carefully. A description of a game of chess suggests political manoeuvring, but it is disrupted and interrupted by formal and expressive twists and turns. In the "gruesome chess, / That endless yayless chess," Omid's view of Iran as a chess board, a field of different political interests and pressures within and outside it, produces a kind of poetry that is far from any kind of unified national sentiment. The translator – Canadian, UK resident, Iranian-descended – also inhabits this diffracted space. The

---

[12] Erín Moure, *O Cidadán* (Toronto: House of Anansi, 2002), 94.

effect of the clashing registers is violent. The neologism "yayless" is itself an unexpected distortion, since it is normally an expression of triumph or encouragement. The OED's earliest citation for "yay" is from 1963, although it is thought to have originated in the States before that. But yay-less is tonally bizarre, held in place here by rhyme with "chess", though that rhyme is not sustained. The game of chess perhaps has echoes of T.S. Eliot's *The Waste Land*; his game of chess in turn is a reference to the Jacobean dramatist Thomas Middleton's *Women Beware Women* – the poem is staged and dramatic in its use of voice, but it also refuses to settle into any single time or place. The dissonance of the translation throughout is central to its effect:

> A yellow parrot out yonder
> Repeated all she said
> In a cold alien cadence:

> "You shan't checkmate me, I know"

The yellow parrot introduces another kind of voice. Mosadeq's note on the translation observes that the parrot's voice is that of the parroting radio, the BBC, which is positioned here, a little archaically as coming from "out yonder". This global arbiter of correct tone in English, dislodged from its hegemonic centrality, is made distant and foreign through the shifting perspective of translation.

While this approach might be viewed in the light of Lawrence Venuti's foreignizing translation, how are we to understand "foreignness"? Is it Iran that is foreign? Or the Cold War machinations of anglophone states? Or the English-language media? Göransson is not convinced by Venuti's argument for foreignizing because, he says it is "a reminder to the English-language reader that the book is in translation, that there is cultural difference. The translation becomes in other words pedagogical." Holding the poem at a critical distance in this way, for Göransson, suggests mastery and superiority, whereas reading and translation can offer more deeply transformative experiences. In his commentary on translating the Swedish poet Eva Kristina Olsson, he refers to the anthropologist Michael Taussig, who in turn draws on Walter Benjamin's essay "The Mimetic Faculty" to describe a "mimetic excess" as a reactive and volatile process that changes the subject.[13] In this "metamorphic sublime", Göransson echoes Olsson's own interests, as revealed in *The Angelgreen Sacrament*, in transformative states: "As the translator, I become the poet, and I become the angel. I become green with luminosity." For Mosadeq, the practice of translation is a means of inhabiting plural identities and remains a dialogue with a still-resonating past; it is productive of transformation while maintaining a critical political stance. What Emily Apter contentiously describes as the "untranslatable"[14] creates, for Mosadeq, the imperative to invent new strategies.

In line with the decision taken in this anthology to focus on the translators and their choices of poets to translate, the reader will notice that two of the poets translated are from Iran, although of different generations and circumstances. Mosadeq's radical approach to translation relies on a certain distance from the author of the source text, but Stephen Watts's translation of Ziba Karbassi is at the other extreme, a co-translation with an Iranian poet resident in the UK. Watts's contribution to the UK's translation culture has been a significant one for many years, spanning several languages. Thanks to the efforts of the Poetry Translation Centre and the journal *Modern Poetry in Translation*, the multiple languages of the UK are represented by mother-tongue translators of poetry, but this has not always been the case. Watts's model of translation as friendship and collaboration is one that has enabled communities of poets to form across languages in a sociality of poetry that extends beyond the translated text itself.

Meena Kandasamy's activist translation, which encompasses fiction and the translation of Dalit poetry, is here focused on a historical text, but one that sustains contemporary injustice. Her work featured here is a rewriting of the third part of *Thirukkural*, from a translation published by Galley Beggar Press as *The Book of Desire* (2023). It is strategic in its critique of forms of oppression that shape contemporary India, but her positioning between India and the UK, where she had moved when we invited her to be part of this anthology, creates an additional charge within her work. In a UK context, it challenges further complacent

---

[13] Michael Taussig, *Mastery of Non-Mastery in the Age of Meltdown* (Chicago, IL: University of Chicago Press, 2020).
[14] Apter, *Against World Literature: On the Politics of Untranslatability*.

assumptions about "tradition" and the kinds of respect it is accorded; as in Kandasamy's own poems, female eroticism is disruptive, not just to the patriarchy but also to the forms of nationhood it underpins. Dan Eltringham's translations of Guatemalan Ana María Rodas's wonderfully titled *Poems of the Erotic Left* offer a different feminist perspective, one which asserts the place of the female body within the revolutionary politics of a resistance movement. Playful in its irony, it exposes the patriarchal views that persist even within the overturning of a political order, creating a revolution within a revolution. Eltringham's translations are, as for many of the translators presented here, not just part of a poetic practice but also part of a wider involvement in international literary networks. The Bristol-based Girasol Press, his joint venture with Leire Barrera-Medrano, publishes poetry in translation and includes the following statement on its website: "We do not draw a distinction here between 'writers' & 'translators', though we may use the terms in reference to specific titles. All creation is re-creation; all re-creation is a first-timer."[15] In this active network, contexts are shaken up, energies reawakened and new possibilities discovered.

It is hard to imagine anyone more immersed in international networks of translation than the prolific Cuban poet Víctor Rodríguez Núñez, whose extraordinary energy and ability to forge connections between like-minded writers, editors and translators has been pivotal to my own understanding of Latin American poetry. We met in 2008 at the Days of Poetry and Wine, which at that time took place in Medana, Slovenia. Poetry's geographies do not map onto states, but the network of poetry festivals that connects Europe often ghosts the lines of older political configurations, inflected (sometimes paradoxically) by the status of culture under Communism and post-Communist national determinations. However, if, as Rodríguez Núñez writes, "the book of political fables / like a cedar in autumn / has lost its proletariat leaves", the ironies of his poems are neither defeatist nor despairing. The "counter-mapping" of Katherine Hedeen's translation becomes a means of asserting new solidarities in place that is multiplied by the specifics of connections between humans and the more-than-human world.

---

[15] https://www.girasolpress.co.uk/authors Accessed 28 August 2022.

It was at the same Slovenian festival that I met Forrest Gander, whose poetry, including his Pulitzer-prize-winning collection *Be With* (New Directions, 2018), likewise articulates a powerful vision of a sociality and way of being in the world that encompasses but also exceeds the human. His translations of Coral Bracho, collected in *It Must Be a Misunderstanding* (Carcanet, 2022), have often traced the mysterious and scintillating contours of bodies and places, forging in the process a language that emerges from both sides of the arbitrary (and quite recent) border separating Mexico from the US. These ecologies of language are continuous with the question raised by the translations presented here: "Which thread is the one that tells our story / and lends us substance / when there's no trajectory / by which to make sense of ourselves?" The "vital thread" of these poems is the gesture of the poem as a connective practice that is extended by translation. Bracho's exploration of the painful circumstances of her mother's dementia becomes an investigation of what holds us in place, what holds us together, even if with strangeness and difficulty. This, too, is a form of counter-mapping, the opposite of the impulse to delineate borders and boundaries.

Proximity does not necessarily imply neighbourliness, and French poetry has had, for many years, a far closer relationship with the poetry of the USA than that of the UK. If this is changing, it is because of the efforts of American translators and UK reception of their translations; French poetry is often encountered transatlantically, as in the magisterial work of Pierre Joris and Jerome Rothenberg, *Poems for the Millennium* (University of California Press, 1997), the first volume of which was my own introduction to the legacy of early twentieth century avant-gardes as they have resonated for US poets. More recently, this is also true of Philip Terry's important anthology *The Penguin Book of Oulipo* (Penguin Classics, 2020). Giving a comprehensive overview of the *Ouvroir de littérature potentielle*, founded in 1960, it marks the contemporary significance of this international group of writers in a UK context, but also charts its synergies with US poetry and includes translations from French by Harry Mathews, Cole Swensen, and Keith and Rosmarie Waldrop, among others. If the distance between the UK and France seems to have increased with Brexit, so too, in this painful loss, has the realization of our connectedness. In translating the poems of Frédéric Forte for this anthology, musical structures drawn from the San Francisco band Deerhoof have provided a point of contact and dissonance, a re-routing of place through a shared transatlantic listening. The mathematical structures of Oulipian procedures are as generative and diffractive when applied to translation as they are in the source text; they offer a means of moving across languages that invites further continuation, as demonstrated by the Outranspo,[16] a translation-focused group that has branched out of the original Oulipo.

Sasha Dugdale's activities as a poet, translator and editor (from 2012 to 2017) of *Modern Poetry in Translation*, have raised the profile of translation in the UK, particularly through her engagement with the work of Maria Stepanova, whose *In Memory of Memory* (Fitzcarraldo Editions, 2021) was shortlisted for the Booker Prize in 2021. Her essay here, its fragmentary form echoing the fragmentation of Stepanova's poetry, places translation within the frame of the poem, of song and memory. Translation does not "represent" a Russian poet, any more than a Russian poet represents "Russia" as an entity or global actor. The translator's mediating, diffractive role emerges in remembered impressions of pine trees, faded paint, incomplete thoughts and anticipation. The translator comes to the poem through her body and experience, making a newly embodied place in the translation, where: "no person is a pane of glass no person is of pure intent no person is devoid of history". The day after I sent the draft version of this anthology to the publishers, Russia invaded Ukraine, and institutions around the world rushed to eliminate Russian works from cultural programming, or to foreground Ukrainian artists. Of course, solidarity with those under attack or exiled is a crucial and much-needed response. However, Stepanova's work, in Dugdale's translation, enables both critical and imaginative resistance to the war's horrifying combination of mental and physical violence. In an article for the *Financial Times*, Stepanova identifies the war as something different from the typical desire of a dictatorship for an expansion of territory, observing, "to my mind this is a special case: there is, behind the movement of Russian military vehicles, a genuine fear of the existence of an Other, a desperate desire to crush this Other, to reform it, ingest it, draw it in, gulp it down, swallow

---

[16] http://www.outranspo.com Accessed 29 August 2022.

it."[17] The splintery deterritorializations of her poetry, and the unresolved spaces that open up in Dugdale's translations, exhibit a radical openness that moves in the opposite direction.

Reading any text is a form of translation, as Moure writes, "because ink and paper, or pixellated light and darkness, are 'read' through a body, an individual apparatus impossible to replicate in terms of its cells and experiences and the ways in which that experience has affected its neural maps and capacities."[18] You, the reader, bring the markings of your own cultural coordinates to bear on the work presented here. Katherine Hedeen's "Afterword" offers counter-coordinates, a Global Positioning System for reading translation with maximum errancy, maximum dissent and wandering. Without a map, we fall back on the body and its intuitions; we learn how these are shaped by the particularities of our location, whether cultural or geographical; we have conversations with strangers.

---

[17] Maria Stepanova, "The war of Putin's imagination" https://www.ft.com/content/c2797437-5d3f-466a-bc63-2a1725aa57a5 Accessed 28 August 2022.
[18] Sophie Collins, *Currently & Emotion: Translations* (London: Test Centre, 2016).

Kareem James Abu-Zeid

Toward a Non-Dual Translational Poetics

Poetry, as we know, is *poesis*, "creation," the making of that which did not exist before.

Poetry, however, is also translation, because no human creation is ever truly *ex nihilo*. Thus, on a deeper level, poetry is always already the translation of certain *somethings* – sensations, feelings, thoughts, images, experiences, traumas, impulses, etc. – into language. These are the sources of the so-called "source" text. In other words, poetry is something that *comes through* the poet.

Translation, too, is creation, *poesis*: the making of that which did not exist before.

A translation is a translation of a pre-existing text, yes. But it is also – in the best of cases – an act of empathy and compassion, i.e., the translation of those certain *somethings* that gave rise to "source" text (which is only a "source" insofar as it relates the subsequent translation). The translator thus – in the best of cases – intuits some of those *somethings* that led to the existence of the "source" text and brings them forth in (a different) language. This intuiting is not an intellectual process, but a certain *sensing* or *feeling into*. It is closer to empathy than to intellectual interpretation. (The intellect certainly has a role to play, however: it comes in later and helps translate the results of this intuiting into language.)

True intuiting or empathy only occurs when the intellect is silent, when the sense or feeling the translator has of existing as a separate self falls away (at least temporarily). Only then is a deeper communion with the sources of the "source" text possible. We could call this communion an empathetic resonance with the "source" text.

In Buddhism, the non-existence of a truly separate self that is endowed with a solid substratum of non-changing existence is the third and final of the three marks/characteristics of existence, and is called *anatta*, i.e., "no separate self" (*an* = no; *atta* = self). In other words, there is no ultimate reality to the seemingly separate self, which is (generally through a prolonged practice of meditation) seen to be comprised of a somewhat arbitrary gathering of thoughts and memories and beliefs that are shoddily held together through the central concept of "I, (insert name here)." Hinduism sometimes attempts to label this phenomenon in more positive terms by declaring that everything is "Self" with a capital "S" (i.e., *Atman* or *Brahman*). But Hinduism, too, in some of its more powerful expressions, is forced to resort to negative terms, and especially: *Advaita Vedanta*, "non-duality," or perhaps more fully and descriptively, "the non-dual ultimate knowledge/realization that is pointed to by the Vedas or that represents the ultimate limit of the Vedas" (my expansive translation). "Non-dual" here points to the experiential realization (rather than the philosophical belief) that the self-world duality is an illusory one. Traditionally, this realization is said to lead to expanded states of peace, well-being, and compassion by transcending the sense of purely *personal* existence. The non-dual teacher Nisargadatta Maharaj has a well-known quote that sums this up: "Love says, 'I am everything.' Wisdom says, 'I am nothing.' Between the two my life flows."

According to a non-dual translational poetics, then, the translator, like the poet, and *as a poet in their own right*, is both nothing and everything. It is good to suspend intellectualization here, and to start to intuit things, as far as that is possible, because this is a space of paradoxes and seeming contradictions.

For example, the present translator might use the self-description "Egyptian-American"; and the poet whose work is presently being translated might use the self-description "Palestinian." This is clearly *something*, and something fairly specific (i.e., "Egyptian-American" and "Palestinian"). Yet both translator and poet are strongly anti-nationalist, and resist facile labels that reduce identity to a specific something (all the while making use of such labels for practical everyday purposes); this is an aspect of the *nothing* spoken of prior, the rejection of any and all labels, of any *essence* that subtends the limiting concepts that must be used. And yet, at the same time, this nothing can give rise to an expansive sense of identity, one that can reach out and embrace *any* identity, as well as multiple (and even seemingly contradictory) identities simultaneously. For example, the poems at hand cross between Europe and Asia, and between the Turkish language and the Arabic one (as embodied by the word *Kadiköy*), before making a further crossing: the transatlantic one, into (a mostly American mode of) English. This is part of the *everything* referenced above. It is only a small part of it, of course, because there are many other crossings we could speak of, including temporal ones.

And so we have, at one and the same time, *something*, *nothing*, and *everything*.

The various crossings referenced above are creative spaces, realms of *poesis*. It is, perhaps, no coincidence that the Arabic word *bahr* means both "poetic meter" and "sea." When we are creating and translating poetry, we are sailing the sea, perhaps many seas, and bringing seemingly disparate realities together. The present translation of poetry (*Kadıköy: Poems*), for example, itself becomes an intersecting point of various semantic and historical matrices: Palestine, Istanbul, Asia, Europe, the US, the Ottoman Empire, etc. Identity can never be reduced to any kind of essence. It is everything, and it is nothing.

Within this multifaceted approach to translation and identity, there is a certain freedom. Various kinds of meditation target the temporary suspension of the conceptualizing/intellectualizing function of the mind, and that same suspension is of immense value to the process of translation. Not only does it allow for a deeper communion with the sources of the "source" text, as mentioned above, it is also a realm of immense creative potential. Paradoxically, out of that silence, unexpected solutions to thorny translational problems can arise – and often with much less effort and struggle and far more satisfying results than when one "racks one's brain" to come up with solutions.

That silent space of awareness can also, by placing meaning and concept in abeyance, lead to greater attention to the bare *sound* of the poetry at hand (both that of the "source" text and the translation). Middling translations of poetry focus primarily on meaning; exceptional ones also pay close attention to the sonic qualities of the texts at hand.

A translational poetics that takes non-duality as its substance-less substratum is difficult to pin down with clear description, yet can have unexpected effects in the practical realm of nitty-gritty translation. To consciously allow a translation to emerge out of the non-dual space of silence is to let go of a good deal of personal agency and volition, and also implies giving oneself over to a non-personal creativity that goes beyond the confines of thought and concept, even as it expresses itself *through* thought and concept. The present essay has been a step toward such a non-dual translational poetics – one that must, necessarily, find embodied form, over and over again, in the actual translation of poetry. In this way, translation itself becomes a mode of meditation, a constantly renewed process of poetic creation.

Najwan Darwish

Translated from Arabic by Kareem James Abu-Zeid

Kadiköy: Poems

Pour the wine, for this age is one of drink,
And the drunkards – they are its noble children.
Elias Abu Shabaki, sung by Nazem al-Ghazali

بيت في "قاضي-كُوْي

تُمْطِرُ على شَبابيكِ بَيْتِكَ في "قاضي-كُوْي
وتُفَكِّرُ أَنَّكَ أَيضاً قاضٍ هارِبٌ
لا يُريدُ أَنْ يَقْضي بشيءٍ
وأَنَّكَ أَيضاً مُحامٍ هارب
لَمْ يَسْتَطِع الدِّفاعَ عن أَيِّ شيء
وأَنَّهُما الآنَ يَلتقيان في قِناعِ شاعرٍ هارِب
في بَيْتٍ هارِب تَنْقُرُ الأَمطارُ شَبابيكَهُ في "قاضي-كُوْي.

29

A House in Kadiköy

It's raining against the windows of your house in Kadiköy[1]
– the village of the qadi –
and you think that you too are a fugitive qadi
who'd rather not issue a single decree,
and that you're a fugitive lawyer, as well,
who couldn't defend anything,
and that these two are meeting, now,
in the mask of a fugitive poet
in a fugitive house, whose windows
are pounded by the rain in Kadiköy.

---

[1] Translator's note: Kadiköy is a district on the Anatolian (Asian) side of Istanbul. The district is famous in Turkey for its liberal character, and used to be home to large numbers of Greeks and Armenians. It was known as Chalcedon, "the city of the blind," during the Ancient Greek period, and was the site of the ecumenical Council of Chalcedon in 451 CE.

A Woman from the Other Side

A woman emerges from memory,
from a day yet to come,
to name the trees for you.

The earth is rippling like oils on a canvas,
it's being painted now.

She's emerging from a dream
and telling you the trees are dreams
in a language they call foreign,
a language they say you've forgotten.

Quickly now, woman –
before men come and cut down the trees.

Out of This Cellar

I told the person whose name I was forced to bear:
Get out of this cellar,
you only ever speak to me in Classical Arabic.
I asked him: How dare you turn every palace
into a cellar where you lay like the Seven Sleepers,
and neither earthquakes nor flames can rouse you?

Open it – open the door
and walk beneath the sky of the Lord.

When I Saw Time

When I saw time repeating itself
at a twist in the road behind one of Jerusalem's hills,
I grew sad. How else
can a person pity time
except by feeling sad?

I could find no meaning in time's repetitions
and the recurrences of fate –
it was simple sorrow, mere repetition,
and my self kept telling me: You've got to break this cycle,
you've got to stand up to the one who declares himself fate
and reject these petty destinies
that keep you running in circles,
you've got to emerge
from compassion into love.

Back then, I was always confused
between pity and something like it,
between love and that which wears a mask.
I was always emerging from all things
and entering into all things
at the very same moment:
gain was no longer gain,
loss no longer loss.
We never used language like that.

My self tells me
that this madness is pointless,
that time's repetitions
lack all meaning,
and all I can do is believe it.

While Sleeping in His New Home

A poet told me that, while sleeping in his new home
– a temporary one, like all his homes –
he saw himself, in a dream,
in the hallways of his old school, from which he'd always escaped,
and from which he'd often been expelled.
That was where he learned to say "No,"
at that school that had tried to break him,
though always he resisted with his sharp tongue,
his hot tears and quick feet –
he always gave them an eye for an eye.
(God, what freedom lies in a young man!)
He told me he dreamed of the school last night:
he was surprised to see that the evil administration
had turned the covers of his last two books into doors for two of
            the classrooms
(the last two he had studied in before they finally succeed in expelling
            him for good).
Each door was the cover of a collection of poetry,
and as he thought of the generations that would go in and out of them
he couldn't understand why he felt a little satisfaction,
for he sensed with his age-old instincts
that this was neither honor nor apology,
but rather a new trick to expel him one last time.

A Thought Occurs

What were our ancestors thinking when they described the breeze
    as gentle?
This is a thought that occurs to me
whenever I'm welcomed by such a breeze…

I'm sitting on a rock in a courtyard
in front of the Church of Aya Efimia,
but the cold soon chases me away.
I must have imagined it – the gentle breeze.

Like Everyone Else

Time wastes you in the ruts of long days.
This is the truth you're running from,
like everyone else.
In the ruts of time the days waste you,
though you imagine it's *you* who's wasting *them*,
here in the ruts of this short life in which you're garrisoned –
a soldier who's lost his war with time
and who's finding it hard
to raise the white flag.

The Day Leaves You

The day leaves you in the carriages of the sun,
which is setting somewhere,
and you've become so used to this
that it no longer hurts.

Night passes near you like some deaf beast
(it has nothing to do with the night
that the singers praise).
It passes near
but does not see you.

It Never Happened Before

I'm neither here
nor there.
This hasn't happened before –
I'm neither in the cup
nor in the voice of the singer.
This city, this sun, these people
are all muddled dreams.

I'm neither here
nor there
and this hasn't happened before –
even the dead must be buried
either here
or there.

I Didn't Know

Happiness was knocking at the door,
but I didn't know it.
I swear it –
I didn't know.

I also didn't know who was knocking
when I opened the door to evil.
I thought it was my aunt, and naively began embracing it.
I was oblivious as I smelled the taint in its heart – I thought it
    was kinship.
I often confused kinship with evil, and didn't know
which one was the other.
And always I opened the door.

I also didn't know who was there
when death came calling,
crying out like a vendor from the streets of my childhood,
crying out in my sleep –
I wake and start running,
but can't catch up with it.

On Half a Wing

I

And I was buried and brought back to life
on half a wing,
in half a day.

II

Sleep was the sweet throe of death,
but how Israfil annoyed me,
calling himself day although it was night,
and – like an employee –
incessantly sounding his horn of Resurrection.

Happiness, in Three Parts

I

The happy ones write everywhere.
I know this,
I was once like them,
I wrote on trees and the walls of caves,
I wrote on the grass,
I wrote with my body,
and on these two hands
the long hair of the days fell gently.

II

The happy ones do not write.
Why should they have to climb the walls of despair in the dark?
Why should they torture themselves by counting the stars?

The happy ones write nothing
but their own happiness.

III

The happy ones do not write
and do not read.

Don Mee Choi

Autogeography=Autotranslation

When I happen to mention to people that I translate contemporary Korean poets, I'm often asked which poets I translate into Korean. Am I to assume that they didn't hear me right? Perhaps I didn't speak loud enough? I've been yelled at by teachers for not speaking English loud enough and sometimes for not speaking at all. What would be a reasonable assumption? English to Korean, or Korean to English? Is translation always direction-specific? Or does direction specificity occur only between certain languages? Am I being unnecessarily unreasonable?

Translation, for me, is inseparable from geography, the geography of a million mines buried across the 38th parallel north, along the DMZ. It's also inseparable from the US imperial war that killed over four million Koreans, mostly civilians. Translation happens for me inside the erased memory – 250,000 pounds of napalm falling daily, rain or snow. Miraculously, my parents survived the war and gave birth to me during the US-backed dictatorship. I grew up as a reasonable child. But because I'm from an unreasonable terrain, autogeography is compulsory for me. It's compulsory for me to translate from Korean to English, rain or snow.

Translation is a Political Act

In 2000, I went to Okinawa, a prefecture of Japan, to participate in a meeting organized by the International Women's Network Against Militarism.[1] At the meeting, I interpreted for the survivors of sexual exploitation at camp towns around US bases in South Korea. I learned from this experience that translation is a political act. That not only our lives are interconnected, but our languages, by histories of imperialism,

---

[1] "2000 Meeting: International Women's Summit to Redefine Security, Okinawa, Japan," The International Women's Network Against Militarization, June 22–25, 2000,http://iwnam.org/what-we-do/international-meetings/2000-meeting-inter-national-womens-summit-to-redefine-security-okinawa-japan/ Accessed 10 May 2021.

colonialism, and the neocolonialism of military and economic warfare. My translation journey and my life journey mirror one another. My mirror life flutters about like an unwelcome sparrow, perpetually homesick.

Twoness

W.E.B. Du Bois observes in *The Souls of Black Folk*: "It is a peculiar sensation, this double-consciousness, this sense of always looking at one's self through the eyes of others…. One ever feels his twoness – an American, a Negro; two souls, two thoughts, two unreconciled strivings; two warring ideals in one dark body…". Du Bois' "twoness" is born out of what he calls a "vast veil": "Then it dawned upon me with a certain suddenness that I was different from the others; or like, mayhap, in heart and life and longing, but shut out from their world by a vast veil."[2]

The *vast veil*, when stretched across the Pacific Ocean, has a different function. The militarization of the *veil* is heightened in order to contain the imagined enemy, perpetuating imperial hegemonic control. The so-called "Manifest Destiny" is woven into every fiber of the *veil*. The *veil* manifests as endless barbed wire fences across the geography of unreasonableness. My twoness is born out of national division. My other is always Red, ready to nuke or be nuked. I translate a poet who was born in the same country I was born in. We essentially grew up in the same house. When I translate Kim Hyesoon, my twin – who still lives in the house I was born in as if I had never left – reaches the poet's house first and waits for my return. My twinness is born out of unreasonable destiny, of distance, of vast homesickness.

Twinness

I think of her as a child. She reminds me, *Don't let your coat weigh you down. There's no winter here. Your luggage will soon absorb the fog.*[3] She barely tolerates my journey from Korea to Hong Kong, from

[2] W.E.B. Du Bois, *The Souls of Black Folk* (New York: Pocket Books, 2005), 6–7.
[3] Don Mee Choi, 'A Journey from Neocolony to Colony,' *The Morning News Is Exciting* (Notre Dame: Action Books, 2010), 81–84.

Hong Kong to the US, from Hong Kong to Germany, from Germany to Australia. She still has my comb, wears my scarf with ribbons and mittens. She remembers my flowered shirt and shorts, a hairpin in my hair. She remembers me as a child. She instructs me to return. She forgets that sparrows never return. Our eternal twoness propels memory and translation. Translation, for me, is a linguistic return. I return to look for her. She still speaks to me in her childish language. She instructs me to translate only the vowels. Sometimes just the consonants:

I erase the ㅇ ㅁ ㅁ consonants from 엄마 ŏmma [mommy] and leave only the ㅓ, ㅏ vowels. ㅓ ㅏ, ㅓ ㅏ, ㅓ ㅏ, ㅓ ㅏ, ㅓ ㅏ, ㅓ ㅏ, ㅓ ㅏ, ㅓ ㅏ, ㅓ ㅏ, ㅓ ㅏ, ㅓ ㅏ[4]

Sometimes I refuse to translate:

무궁화꽃이피었습니다
무궁화꽃이피었습니다
무궁화꽃이피었습니다
무궁화꽃이피었습니다[5]

Radical Twin

In 1999, I translated for Korean activists a short report on one of the women I met near a US military base in Dongducheon, which is now closed. Nearly all the US bases are being consolidated into two massive bases in the central part of South Korea and not along the border. Empire's target is China, not the usual suspect, North Korea. This is what "the American strategic pivot to Asia"[6] looks like. South Korea is one of the most convenient places on earth to install and signal the New Cold War because the old Cold War never ended on the peninsular. In military language, such base-rich neocolonial territory is referred to as

[4] Kim Hyesoon, "Bird Rider," *Phantom Pain Wings*, trans. by Don Mee Choi.
[5] Don Mee Choi, *Hardly War* (Seattle & New York: Wave Books, 2016), 10.
[6] Kenneth Lieberthal, "The American Pivot to Asia," *FP*, December 21, 2011, https://foreignpolicy.com/2011/12/21/the-american-pivot-to-asia/. Accessed 18 May 2021.

a "Lily Pad."

> Another mysterious death of a GI's woman. She had bled pro-
> fusely, and dark spots were found all over her body. Her face
> was flat against the floor with her tongue protruding. Her
> landlady called the police because she hadn't seen her tenant for
> several days. What kind of work did she do?[7]

I use my neocolonial language for translation. It's also my language
of resistance. There's always two of us. I must speak as a radical twin.

Tranceness

T.J. Clark opens his essay "Aboutness"[8] on Hieronymus Bosch's
"Terrestrial Paradise" by embedding himself in the naked man with a
tonsure. Clark channels his voice and thoughts, writing as an embodied
art critic:

> An angel in red stands next to me. The crowd on the other side
> of the angel appear to be simple folk – I'm not priding myself
> on my tonsure and Roman nose – but they too are focused on
> the light from above … I myself have no memory of having
> just exited from the earth. (Uprightness is my natural element.
> I stand tiptoe on two small feet.)

Then he breaks out of his self-induced trance:

> Obviously, it is a device, and not without dangers, to put the
> particulars and uncertainties of Bosch's panel into the mind of
> one of its protagonists. But it is not a device – it is a necessity…

Such device or necessity, putting myself into the minds of the many
protagonists of Kim Hyesoon's poetry, is a frequent phenomenon for

---

[7] Choi, "Diary of Return," *Morning News*, 18.
[8] T.J. Clark, "Aboutness," *London Review of Books* 43, no. 7 (2021), 6.

me. In "Pig Pigs Out"[9] no angel is standing next to me. I'm standing among other pigs: *snuggly Pig, cozy Pig, XXXL Pig, pork Pig.* Contrary to popular belief, pigs rarely have the time to sit, lollygagging around. There's no such thing as leisure for our kind, for we are forced to pig out constantly. However, *Pigs all have the same name.* I'm *Pig9.* My short curly tail happens to resemble a number 9, a sign that I'm a pious *Pig.* As for my pig nose, it's best left undescribed. My teeth have been pulled out already, so whenever I oink at the heavenly sky, *my tongue is lonely all by itself.* We are in high demand on earth because in 2003 the import of US beef has been banned due to mad cow disease. However, foot-and-mouth disease is ravaging our kind. Humankinds bury us alive. They dump us into trenches by the truckloads. We stand tiptoed on our small feet, crying. Poet Kim Hyesoon writes about us in relation to the way humankinds have also ravaged other humankinds during the dictatorship – a nameless disease. The translator standing next to me is in a revery of some sort:

(돼지= twaeji=Pig) + (뒈지=tweji=die) + (뒈지는 돼=dying Pig=dead Pig=pig out Pig) + (뒈지는 돼지는 돼지라고 생각하는 뒈지는 돼지다=dying   Pig thinks dying Pig is Pig) = (Pig who pigs out thinking that Pig who pigs out is Pig)

Pigness is my device. I'm necessarily Pig. My radical twin with a hairpin in her hair stands next to me … *I myself have no memory having just exited* from Korea.

Lilymethod

In "IS THERE WHITE LIGHT FOR US?" Kim uses a conjoined word 백합질식사시키는.[10] The literal translation is lilyasphyx-iationmake. I translated it as lilyasphyxiating," then revised it to "lilyphyxiating." I removed the kidney-resembling *a*. Such precise removal requires what

[9] Kim Hyesoon, "I'm OK, I'm Pig," *Sorrowtoothpaste Mirrorcream*, trans. Don Mee Choi (Notre Dame, IN: Action Books, 2014), 75–79.

[10] Kim Hyesoon, *Nalgae hwansangt'ong* [*Phantom Pain Wings*] (Seoul: Munhakkwajisŏngsa, 2019), 162.

translators like to call skill. I prefer to call it lilymethod. Lilymethod also involves listening intently to Kim Hyesoon's bird language in her new collection *Phantom Pain Wings*. It took about a lilyyear for me to learn the bird language, and I even grew a pair of lilyyears in the process. I can totally identify with the man with a bird in Clark's trancelation, though the man appears to be earless:

> A man to my left is absorbed in conversation with a grey and white bird. It looks as if he is instructing the creature – his fingers, like those of the rough theologian, are didactic ... Or is the man taking lessons from the bird?

From where I am, which is nowhere significant – peeking out of a bush, the man is talking with his hands. It must be his lilymethod. His fingers are as pointed as the bird's beak, and his modest nose suggests that he may have been a translator on earth at some point. The bird is instructing the man to use his hands to transmit its language. Naturally, foreign language calls for hand gestures, the universal finger-pointing, and certainly finger-flipping at times of ultra-terrestrialism. Bird's message is transferred from hand to hand, fluttering forever upward to the fountain of birds. Bird's incessant chatter is nobody's business, but once translated into a cacophony of hands, it becomes everybody's business:

> You were born inside bird
> Not opposite of that
> You died inside bird
> Not opposite of that
> You were born and died[11]

How the man came to lose his ears may be another story, unrelated to his prior occupation. But I suspect they are related because the loss of ears and loss of years are sonically and physiologically related. My hearing is muffled, frayed, in disarray by the sound of my own heartbeat as my ears flutter back and forth from nowhere to the unreasonable

---

[11] Kim Hyesoon, *Nalgae hwansangt'ong* [Phantom Pain Wings] (Seoul: Munhak-kwajisŏngsa, 2019), 162.

terrain, inducing DMZ dizziness. *Lily Pad* must go! is all I can utter with my hands. From where I am, a translator's ears must be ever ready to shift from lilyears to lilyyears, or even pigears. *Not opposite of that.* My ears must remain in flight within and without the *veil,* the hailing napalm, the vertigo of language. *Not opposite of that.* Liliness is a must, rain or snow.

Birds I seeded inside your body feel all lumpy – you must

Your blood is replaced with bird's blood – you must
. . . .

Like the way your throat is parched from thirst,

your body's birds combust – you must
. . . .
Birds inside you glimmer – you must

Kim Hyesoon

Translated from Korean by Don Mee Choi

from I'm OK, I'm Pig!

Pig Pigs Out

It's Pig, Pig who has never seen the outside, always Pig, depressed Pig, Pig who cries wolf, Pig who has chosen the most terrified pig in the world to be the king, Pig who shouts Oh, fantastic sewer! while hugging its pillow, Pig who laughs alone hoping mommy will get arrested, mommy who gave birth to Pig who will pig out till it drops dead, Pig with bloated lips who thinks the whole world is rice porridge, it's XXXL Pig, Pig who takes up the entire bed, its name can only be Pig, shivering-shivering Pig whenever it hears Cross the ocean, yes-yes Pig who has never once raised its head, Pig who pigs out from fear when it looks up at the vast night sky, Pig who pigs out thinking that Pig who pigs out is Pig

Droopy front and back limbs Pig, oinks with its tail tucked between its legs Pig, air is bundled up but why is it so heavy Pig, smells like a steaming cloud when you put your hand in its armpit Pig, unbelievably soft Pig, ultimately snuggly Pig, play all your life riding on me Pig, rats gnaw on piglets yet cozy Pig, what have you stuffed into your eyes Pig, why doesn't Pig know that it's Pig Pig, a photograph knows a mirror knows only you don't know Pig, never has looked out a window Pig, teeth pulled Pig, sigh Pig, regret Pig, after its teeth are pulled out and its tail cut off its tongue is lonely all by itself in its mouth Pig, but whenever it opens its mouth makes pig pig sounds Pig, pork Pig

qqqq   the sound of Pig crying along with a crow perched on its head
qqqq   naturally it's Pig screaming when its owner goes to jail and piss and shit rises up to Pig's knees

qqqq the words that Pig yells inside when it denies being Pig

qqqq the words that Pig utters You're Pig when you turn around to look at your mommy being taken away

qqqq most of all, the squeals of our nation's pigs that don't know that I'm Pig

Bloom, Pig!

Has to die even if it didn't steal
Has to die even if it didn't kill
Without a trial
Without a whipping
Has to go into the pit to be buried

Black forklifts crowd in
No time to say Kill! Kill!
No time for the blood to splatter onto the shit-smeared walls or light bulbs
No time for the piglets just popped out from the stomach to get skinned and made into cheap colorful shoes

No time for the pale-faced interrogator wearing dark sunglasses to yell Fess up! Fess up!
No time to gamble with terror as if skipping rope, whether I can survive the torture or not
No time to bite the flesh of my mouth as if biting the hand that's hitting my friend's cheek in the next room
No time to tie up hands and feet and pull my head back and force water into me
No time to say Mommy please forgive me, I was wrong, I won't do it again
No time to put a towel over my face and pour water from a pot
No handcuff or strap

Every night I read my country's history of torture
Then in the morning I open the window and sing loudly at the roofs
below the mountain
How could I possibly forget this place?
I have Pig who needs to be rinsed with a song then go
Dear Song, Please stay stuck to my body for 12 hours

A horde of healthy pigs like young strong men get thrown into the pit

They cry in the grave
They cry standing on two legs, not four
They cry with dirt over their heads
It's not that I can't stand the pain!
It's the shame!
Inside the grave, stomachs fill with broth, broth and gas

Stomachs burst inside the grave

They boil up like a crummy stew
Blood flows out the grave
On a rainy night fishy-smelling pig ghosts flash flash
Busted intestine tunnel their way up from the grave and soar above
    the mound
A resurrection! Intestine is alive! Like a snake!

Bloom, Pig!
Fly, Pig!

Boars come and tear into the pigs
A flock of eagles comes and tears into the pigs

Night of internal organs raining down from the sky!
Night of flashing decapitated pigs!
Fearful night, unable to discard Pig even if I die and die again!
Night filled with pig squeals from all over!

Night of screams, I'm Pig! Pig!

Night when pigs bloom dangling-dangling from the pig-tree

from Phantom Pain Wings

IS THERE WHITE LIGHT FOR US?

Bundle of rags under the dining table

Wings are bunched up
as if gasping

I want to be cool like the cold birds of the winter sky

But my hands tremble, for I despise my family so much
Every time I breathe, rags heave up and down

Flickering sound
Crashing sound
Apologetic houses everywhere

I keep having dreams about a bird under my older brother's heel

Over there, tiny Mommy is under someone's heel, but I can't go and
    rescue her

Girl wraps the rags with her clothes and coddles them
That girl can't be me

In the morning I brush my teeth hard, but they didn't turn white

I wonder whether my bones are white even if I don't brush them

White Vindu Chakra from Daddy
Red Vindu Chakra from Mommy
Raw meat dyes my teeth daily
I steal a candle from a temple
I think about lighting my apologetic house up white
Smell of the Tibetan temple I've visited
Smell of shiny floors like all the faces at the temple
Smell of flesh stuck to bones

I think I've reached the top, dragging up my wings
but when I turn around there is no mountain
Ah, the dreadful white mountain is gone
Color white's dormant period is brief
I write a letter from the flattened mountain,
You're going to become filthy for sure
Damn mountain! How dare you perform the color white?

You died far faraway and returned
Daddy, like an owl,
you perch on the dining table
and see night during the day
night during the night

Daddy, when you're too embarrassed
you swear every other word
like I swear at myself in the third person

Everybody says it's my fault
and not my brother's fault

Daddy, your flesh-colored head
spews white hair like a white trumpet

Older brother's flesh-colored head
spews black hair like a black trumpet

Sin redder than blood becomes whiter than snow
Jesus the master washer is on Mommy's lap, giving a sermon
Jesus, Mommy's Jesus, you raise up so many lilies
Jesus, you are lilyphyxiating Mommy!

Bundle of rags under the table
Girl spews rags like a rag trumpet

My body has no color white
I don't perform color white

Bird's Repetition

All the stories bird tells perched on the treetop are about me
Nothing about the rumors of my lies, my thefts and such but
something ordinary like how I was born and died
Bird talks only about me even when I tell it to stop or change the topic
It's always the same story like the sound of the high heels of the
    woman, walking around in the same pair all her life
This is why I have a bird that I want to break

Like a poet who buys a ream of A4 paper
and crumples the sheets one by one and tosses them
I have a bird I want to break
When I crumple up my poems that are like
the family members inside a mirror in front of me
I can hear the stories of fluttering birds
"You were born and died"
Then I say, "You scissormouths" and
go buy a paper shredder
to shred every poetry book of mine
But later, when I opened up the shredder

a flock of birds was sitting inside, talking about me as if reading
    line by line
Moreover, each bird had a different face
and the hens talked about me even while sitting on their eggs
They didn't even care to fly off
Instead, they clustered under the peanut tree and talked about me
like peanuts under the ground
So, I said to them, enough of telling the same old story of how I was
    born and died
How about something else?
For instance, how about the fact that I always wear the same high heels
    to work and back
but when I'm under the same tree at the same park
I always dance a waltz
And do several movements of embracing the moon
But they replied,
You were born inside bird
Not opposite of that
You died inside bird
Not opposite of that
You were born and died

찬란했음 해 (Glimmer — You Must)

네 몸에서 내가 씨를 심은 새들이 울퉁불퉁 만져졌음, 해
네 피가 새의 피로 새로 채워졌음, 해
네 발걸음이 공중으로 경중경중 디뎌지는 나날
바보 멍청이 네가 네 몸의 문을 찾지 못하는 나날
내가 되고 싶은 네가 네 몸에서 나가고 싶어 안달했음, 해
습한 여름에도 발아래 땅이 한없이 멀어지는 그런 가을이 온 것
    같고
네 목구멍이 목마름으로 타들어 가듯
네 몸의 새가 타올랐음, 해
키득키득 네 입술 밖으로 연기가 새어 나오고
내 몸에 앉고 싶은 새가 더 더 더 달아오르는 나날
쿵쿵 울리는 심장의 둥지에서
쿵 소리 한 번에 새 한 마리씩
미지근한 네 두 눈의 창문 밖으로 언뜻언뜻 아우성치는 새들이
    엿보이는
그런 나날
불불듯 날개가 크게 돋아났는데도 돌 속인 그런 나날
가슴 위에 얹은 네 오른손이 마치 네 엄마처럼
새들로 꽉 찬 네 가슴을 지그시 누르고
매일 그런 자세로 나를
네 안의 새들이 찬란했음, 해

Glimmer — You Must

Birds I seeded inside your body feel all lumpy — you must

Your blood is replaced with bird's blood — you must

Every day, your footsteps stompstomp up in the air

Every day, idiotic, stupid you can't find the door to your own body

You who wants to become me became frantic to leave your body —
    you must

It's a muggy summer, but the ground below feels endlessly distant like
    autumn

Like the way your throat is parched from thirst

your body's birds combust — you must

Puffs of smoke leak from your lips

and birds that want to perch on my body become hot hot hotter by
    the day

Bam bam inside your heart's nest

a single beat for each hatchling

The day I glimpse howling birds outside the windows of your
    lukewarm eyes

The day wings quickly sprout, but they're inside the rock

Like your mommy, your right hand

gently pushes down on your chest filled with birds

You do that to me every day in same position

Birds inside you glimmer — you must

Sasha Dugdale

if earth

Start with blankness and fill the page slowly.

Sometimes over weeks.

It wasn't the right phrase   but it reminded me that my mind
was as usual occupied with words.

I think so much all the time and I think half-thoughts, thoughts
never brought to fullness because I carry them around and the perfection of a thought is in its utterance, its release from the body

is everyone rushing about with their unstable thoughts?

(but for translation I do not need to utter these thoughts oh I can
clothe them in other words)

and do we have our own thoughts or are we not like the entangled
canopies of trees? their high burden shared?

The hoardings have broken away from the wall to reveal the letters
of the sign in negative
the paint less faded
where they were fixed

drawing back from the scene, refusing it, and yet seeing it unfold
like a length of drugget: this drawing-out of the final revelation has
its biochemical effect

how can I translate until
this biochemical effect

and how it has changed me
anticipation and completion
reader, and creator in its wake

SPEAKER: the village is invisible from the hills because there are
so many trees lining the roads, the buildings simply disappear into
woodland (pause) and you can't see the passing of time in the same –

LISTENER: but it isn't true that it's a timeless landscape. The
original Scots pine copses on the greensand all went a century ago,
only a few remained in my childhood, scattering their dry hat pins,
and I gazed up at these on my way to school and imagined Russia

I stand against this idea of translation as a vitrine in which we
see the original. I stand against it here, me, many kilos of proteins,
lipids, water, with a slow local history of my own composition and
concurrent decomposition (I see also that it is a grave act to scribble
in these lines)

no person is a pane of glass no person is of pure intent no person
is devoid of history

SPEAKER: so my translation of this piece grows uninterruptedly
from a small foot stepping on dry needles, a head looking up at the
top-heavy pines and the summer-blue sky and imagining another
country, a country without shape or colour or form, all made of
anticipation

*

language plants growing from rapidly-changing soils but like the
Pot of Basil in reverse, plants fragrant non-native plants have set
their roots in my cerebellum

xiv.

Did unknown hands touch? I stretch out and –
Snake-like it convulses (means we touched lightly)
Or chirrups like a swallow
(means we didn't touch)

*

1. Maria Stepanova's "If Air" is a response to, or perhaps an echo of, Gennady Aygi's folk variations.

2. Aygi, a poet born in the Chuvash Republic during the Soviet period, who spoke and composed poetry in both Russian and his own Chuvash language, wrote a collection of variations on folk poetry from the Volga region, including from his own native language.

3. The sequences in his book are numbered four-line stanzas, with the feel of tiny fragments

4. In "If Air" Maria takes her formal shape from Aygi's variations, as well as her epigraph.[1]

5. While Maria adheres to the form and feel of these fragments, which are mysterious and often concerned with the faint line between living and spirit world, she says her own fragments place contemporary solidity against the spiritual world

a landscape of car parks, phone boxes, building sites, driving through old villages on the roadside

---

[1] when we translate, we lift a piece out of its natural environment, like a creature we deprive it of its progenitors, and we are unable even to guarantee descendants in its new habitat. I see the process almost bodily, the text in my hand, trailing roots and fronds – translation, accompanied by that squealing wrenching sound – translation with a knife to saw away at what holds the poem in its earth – translation as deracination.

v.

Her shadow still behind the same fence
but go back tomorrow and you won't find her
then in you
her shape will have entered forever

of course death is deeply local: see my father's body his self so absolutely gone what a strange thing to see the casing like that in a coffin in the backroom of the village undertaker's and

how he appeared in my dreams and wanted to talk

xi.

only in my dreams
can I enter our yard
be still, my beloved dog
oh you, my tawny nightingale

place that memory alongside another, a sweltering day, another father, this time in a sagging cardboard coffin which lay at our feet, the lid aslant as we drove out to the cemetery on Moscow's ring road in a jangling funeral bus

xxxvii.

A while now you've not been here
but lines of your face, expressions
flash across meadows and woods
scattered over the faces, backs, shoulders
of your great-grandchildren and grandchildren

The fifth stanza of "If Air" is not a translation in the way a reader might imagine translation to be. In Russian it is a four-line sensual game with the word нежить, perhaps rendered most literally as 'un-dead'. But the same word is also the verb 'to caress' – and if taken apart into its constituent parts: 'not-to-inhabit'.

What would you do in such a case?

I wrote the word 'wight' and from it stretched my hand into white reflectiveness

This sort of translation is closer to jazz improvisation: on another day I would chose spirit and level up differently; on a third day I would weave in the wee folk. But to continue the improv metaphor, is my interlude in the same key? does it follow the same musical structures? or do I align my soul with the line, asking you trust me –

perhaps you can't trust me.
                then what are you reading

    your intimate experience: you gazing through the pane of glass
    at the original in the cabinet

If you are startled then perhaps yes something chemical has happened

I wrote the words I didn't write the words I wrote
The words I didn't write
The words I wrote
The words I didn't

Am I influenced by the poems I translate? I put my voice, all its long roots its many tubers at the disposal of the text. Do they influence me or do I influence them?

When I give them an English shape do they become English assimilate or do they act upon English does it change does its atomic weight increase?

If I see voice as a line through time, rather than a moment in time, then the idea of influence worries me less

    two voices align in places
    and those places are mysterious
    like the places where the living and the dead adjoin

    I can't predict them
    although I reach
       for them

    x.

    bright and then dark with the singing in the house
    as if our breathing had made
    meadows of warmth
    hang above our heads

                  *

(verses in italics are draft translations of fragments of Gennady Aygi's variations on Volga folk music, chosen by Maria Stepanova)

Maria Stepanova

Translated from Russian by Sasha Dugdale

ЕСЛИ ВОЗДУХ

1.

Нежная ты, дорожная грязь:
Обращалась к каждой ноге
За простым увереньем
И за печатью – к лапе

2.

Только самые кроны
Ходят волнуясь туда-сюда,
В ветках закат, в ноге и вокруг
Уже глубокая ночь

3.

Вот, мне приснилось, что мне
Скатали как старый ковер, мое
Унесли, я развесили на заборе.
Тычется в руки ничей присо

A birch by the name of Alexander
Gennady Aygi

If Air

1.

Tenderest dirt
You enjoin each foot
To the simplest bond
And each paw – to its seal

2.

Only the crowns
Agitated, move this way and that
Dusk in the branches, but at the foot
And around: darkest night

3.

I dreamed that I
Was rolled up like an old carpet
Me was carried away, I hung out on the fence
Nobody's dream presses itself into the hands

4.

I dreamed that a corner
Filled with dust, with cat hair
With crumbs of plasticine
Rolled itself into a corner

5.

I dreamed that the wight
Didn't know what to think itself:
Translucent – or transcendent
Creature or reflected light?

6.

The black corner wishes itself red
The firebird fizzles to blackbird
And the white one is fortunate:
It was forest, then tried at being smoke

7.

It's late, let's sleep.
To the left of us and to the right
The candles gutter in their lanterns
On neighbouring graves

8.

You twist, you turn
But sleep won't come, and under your left shoulder
Where the cliff drops away to the Volga
A path has been trodden through you to the mud

9.

Heavy river, ice-bearing
On the left, but now you cross into barren land
From here until that bush:
And thereafter – it's no longer you

10.

If you became air, don't the high branches
Tickle when you pass through?
If fire, may you never lack for feed.
If earth, may the sky bed you softly.

11.

Ears are hidden between one paw and the other
From ear to ear the animal brain
Driven into a dark corner flaps its flippers
Searches its way out into the watery mass

12.

The outlines of phone boxes and water pumps
Have long been lost to the air
That thing glimmering in the sun's last rays –
You must have imagined it

14.

Look at these letters
How fine the writing! What it says is
Unimportant: with every loop, every bold line
You say yes to her

15.

At the dacha in Saltykovka
The butterfly marks the living
With a single touch
To tell them apart

16.

Hold your shape, neither curdling nor softening
You won't make it home, back to milk
Packet of farm butter
In its splendid greaseproof wrap

17.

I dreamed again:
In the corner of a small square
The cobbles called you
As I walked on them

18.

And I dreamed
That you came to the fair in town
And we sat at long tables
And what's so surprising about that?

19.

I can't look you in the face
Not because it is too bright
Nor because I am ashamed
Nor because it isn't there

20.

Don't imagine everyone is wandering about naked
Just a little crystalline –
Girls with see-through braids
Down to their see-through pants

21.

The grey branch creeps along the railings
Like a cat, a dog skittering down the path like
The wind, and only hearing is soundless
Equal to nothing, never equalled.

22.

Dig a hole and lie face down in the earth
Tell it I love you and cover immediately
With your flat palm keep it warm
And wait for the bitter mushroom to grow

23.

Barren river, sans people
Sans wind and water
Bare pointer of movement
But pointing nowhere in particular

24.

We hid away from the rain under a stone.
World stopped briefly to dry itself
Come crawling out, my eye-less friend –
Its wheels are not meant for us
Today

25.

The wood is dark enough by itself
Twist and turn, turn and twist –
Patient friction will bring on light
Before dawn

26.

Building site, and beyond a car
Park, and beyond that a trail of light
Hold it back, like a hand grasping
Another hand time for home

27.

Walked a little way felt weary
Looked about sat down caught breath
Sat a while longer caught cold
Shifted his weight died was resurrected

28.

Old village
We just drove though
Blue framed windows
Moss-green coals

29.

The unresolved disputes
Circulate over the hundred-year-old
battlefield
Horsefly and horse, hawk and mouse

30.

Where are you, tell me?
Your freezing water, stream
Drags you south
By the hair

31.

In that once-upon-a-time house
The lamp and the drapes
Radiated such light
That our dark seems darker

32 (a).

And the little round cloud
And the pine grove and hills and road
No longer pretend
That they are not you

32 (b).

And the little round cloud
And the pine grove and hills and road
Expose you more every day
Soon you will be quite divested – and I will see

32 (c).

And the pine grove and the cloud and the road
Is it their job to restrain you?
When they twitch in pain
Your features flare and are extinguished

33.

I walk and speak
With you
And with you.
There, see – we talked.

34.

And now
Let's try to breathe with the whole chest

Breathe out
And in
And now we'll all withdraw
Each to his own
To catch our breath

And again
And once more

Dan Eltringham

Translating the Erotic Left: On Ana María Rodas

I came to translating the Guatemalan poet Ana María Rodas as part of a research process, rather than as a "translator" – a side-avenue in poetic practice to my current work on the translation of Latin American militant poetries. As I began translating the magnificently entitled *Poemas de la izquierda erótica* (Testimonio del Absurdo Diario, 1973), a volume that scandalised Guatemalan polite society when it was first published in 1973, I suppose I was just trying to find something out: about the social world adjacent to the guerrilla in Guatemala, and about the 1970s and the challenge posed to Guevara's "New Man" by feminist critique. Derrida says that translators are the only ones who know how to read, or that translating is the only true reading and writing. I don't know about that, but translating Rodas sprang, for me, from that sort of an impulse: translation as a mode of close reading and enquiry.

The "erotic left" takes aim at the *machista* culture of Latin American revolutionary movements as Rodas experienced them, which lines up with Ileana Rodríguez' critique, in *Women, Guerrillas, and Love* (1996), of the post-Cuban, "heroic" guerrillas, in which women were figured in highly schematic terms. In *Women & Guerrilla Movements* (2002) Karen Kampwirth notes that while the Cuban Revolution of 1959 and the *foco*-theory guerrillas it inspired in the early 1960s were largely male affairs, by the end of the decade and into the 1970s, female participation in what were increasingly mass mobilizations of society expanded hugely. Shifting socio-economic factors made armed struggle more of an option or outcome for Latin American women after around 1965, who in some cases left traditional gender roles behind when they joined the guerrilla. These histories have been slow in becoming known. Margaret Randall's tireless advocacy for an insurgent feminism challenged the Cuban then Nicaraguan revolutionary processes from within in terms of gender equality; while her recent translations of the Bolivian poet and guerrilla Rita Valdivia, who was killed in Cochabamba in 1969 at the age of 23, recuperate the wildly strange work of a female militant writing in the hermetic avant-garde tradition.

Alert to such aporia in the canons of commitment and transnational solidarity that coalesced in the 60s and 70s, my attention was drawn by Rodas's sardonic title, *Poems of the Erotic Left*, suggestive of the kind of fraught-yet-friendly satire that was scarce in militant verse of the period. Rodas is a member of what is known as the "irreverent generation" in Guatemalan letters, referring to those who lived as children during the brief period of revolutionary democracy that was ended by the CIA-sponsored coup of 1954. Unlike many of her committed and artistic friends, Rodas stayed in Guatemala for the whole period of the armed conflict (1960–1996), at its worst during the dark days of the 1980s when death squads committed genocidal reprisals against Maya communities accused of assisting the guerrillas. Rodas – who sympathised with the struggle but never took up arms herself – remained in Guatemala City working as a journalist, associating with painters more than writers. As a "*guerrillera* of love," the sexual politics of the Catholic family and their replication within revolutionary relationships were openly challenged by Rodas's ambiguous self-positioning, both supportive and critical of the armed struggle, "somewhere / around there as on the erotic left."

The first poem by Rodas I found was posted on a blog, with the verse lineation taken out, so it read as a paragraph: in my translation, "You do well, great maestro. I am the *guerrillera* in your regime, the object that rises up with weapons of love [...]." At first I thought it was a prose exposition of the poems excerpted from *Poems of the Erotic Left* that were pasted below: a statement of poetics and politics, perhaps. When I managed to find a copy of the book, republished by Madrid press papelesmínimos in 2019, I put the lineation back together, reconstructing Rodas's deft movement between indented phrase, sense and enjambment, all couched in the second-person direct address that can't help but identify you – the reader, perhaps the translator – with the double standards of an emancipatory politics premised on patriarchal power plays, with the "regime" of "well-ordered" affect, and bodies in their place.

This "dictatorship" of love is the main object of *Poems of the Erotic Left*, which reclaims the body as a territory of struggle with its frank treatment of sexuality and power. Rodas uses a clearly demarcated voice, a verbal construct I sought to replicate in English, as a male translator with a responsibility to the feminist politics of the poems. While I am generally sceptical of the entropic fidelity paradigm that continues to be a popular way of thinking about loss and gain in poetry translation, I also see respect and recreative invention as relative and positional, and in this case I very definitely did not wish to overlay my own rhythms and tonalities any more than is inevitable in the process of re-sounding out line and syntax.

But anyway, despite their excoriating direct address, shockingly intimate content (for the time) and tonal consistency, these poems sabotage the fake naturalization of self and person implicit in the creative writing injunction to "find your voice" by overloading and fragmenting information about the poet's physical body-with-organs. Personal history beginning with birth is expressed by enumeration that is a record of accretion and subtraction: "3 daughters and 2 dogs come along with me / what's left of 2 marriages [...] I've got a liver, stomach, 2 ovaries, a womb, heart and brain, plus accessories." As Johannes Göransson observes in *Transgressive Circulation* (Noemi Press, 2018), finding one's voice is a kind of necrotic Neoplatonic summoning that privileges spirit over body, but which cannot account for the material remainder of that body's residual presence in the voice, as molecular disturbance and morphemic slippage, reminding the reader of the corporeality and decay concealed by the fiction of textual stability and authority. Derrida again: translation is like one language licking or caressing another, like a tongue or/of flame, a desiring proximity and distance (difference) in which they appear to touch without complete consummation. Translation's proliferative versioning further undoes the binary equivalence of origin to copy, a patrilinear, genetic way of thinking about authorship, influence, inheritance and debt that ringfences multiple rewritings of texts within the enclosure of copyright.

As it happens, around the time I began – idly, as a distraction from "writing" – to translate Rodas, my research threw up Zoë Anglesey's translation of the same poem I had encountered as prose and later translated, not knowing that hers existed. Anglesey, who died in 2003, was a poet, editor and jazz writer, perhaps best known for her 1982 collection *Something More Than Force: Poems for Guatemala, 1971–1982* (Adastra Press), which gives a harrowing account of the death squads and disappearances that scarred Guatemala's counterinsurgent countryside. Her version of this poem was issued as a broadside prospectus for an anthology she edited for Granite Press in 1987, *Ixok Amar-Go: Central American Women's Poetry for Peace/Poesía de mujeres centroamericanas por la paz*. Designed by Bea Gates, the broadside sets Rodas's poem alongside Anglesey's translation, against a tiled background of four Guatemalan women wearing traditional huipils. These Maya women were, the broadside implies, *Granddaughters of Corn*, in the title of the book in which the image was later included, published by the radical left publisher Curbstone Press in 1988.

Anglesey's version of the poem is different from mine in lots of ways. Her title is *Poems from the Erotic Left*, and elsewhere it is listed as *Poems from the Erotic Front* (I don't know whether this is an earlier draft of the title). Either way, the prepositions are doing similar, if not identical work, but "front" is an intriguing departure: one can imagine a guerrilla-esque acronym for the People's Erotic Liberation Front, or FPLE (Frente Popular de Liberación Erótica). This is not my joke, or indeed even a joke at all. After the Nicaraguan Revolution in 1979, a group of feminists set up the Partido de la Izquierda Erótica, a political party that wins election after election in the Nicaraguan poet of revolutionary desire Gioconda Belli's novel *El país de las mujeres* (*The Country of Women*, La Otra Orilla, 2010). Of course, I am necessarily and rightly excluded from some of the experiential ground of these poems, and in making direct comparison between our choices I don't wish to suggest anything other than the richness of translation's structural imprecision, or the impossibility of "rightness" as selection opens out to variegation inflected by a multitude of factors: identity, experience, historical moment, place, how diction is shaped by the shifting sands of politics.

In the poem itself, Anglesey translates "maestro" as "teacher"; I prefer to keep the loan-word for its connotations of high-handedness. I think her "under" [your regime] is probably better than my "in" in the second line, but I'd rather preserve the difference now that I've seen both. She takes "jornada" as "journey," – the day's progress, sojourn – whereas I wanted to suggest the refusal or sabotage of labour, and of care-work in particular, so I went for "shift." In the second stanza, I pulled the adverb of the opening imperative, "Rastrea bien," right down into the third line, inserting it into the injunction to "aplasta sin escrúpulos," which becomes "quash *well* and without scruple," I suspect because I liked the sound and rhythm of this alliterative and phrasal parallelism. Anglesey's "bud of subversive tenderness" is for me a "shoot," which again I suppose my subconscious selected because of its double meaning in the context of armed struggle. But I don't know, because I hadn't thought about it, or really any of these selections very much, until sitting down to write this comparison. This not-knowing, for me, is the best argument in favour of Göransson's impure, promiscuous poetics of translation as multiplicitous joy-in-difference, which is messy and imperfect, like our bodies and selves.

In that spirit, I'll end with an image from my translation of *Poems of the Erotic Left* that embodies some of the contradictions of what I'm thinking of as "militant fun," which carla bergman and Nick Montgomery explore in *Joyful Militancy* (AK Press, 2017) in allusion to the Italian anarchist Alfredo Bonanno's 1977 polemic *Armed Joy*. The book explores the potentialities of "subversive tenderness" within radical movements that have become codified by internal tyrannies and anxieties. For Rodas, *un trago de ron*, interwoven pleasure and decay, sex and excess, make up the nihilistic, utopian drive of "machine-gun / desire":

> The rum sinks noisily into the throat
> – 10,000 dead cells –
> and machine-gun
> desire
> in the fingers.

Ana María Rodas

Translated from Spanish by Dan Eltringham

Machine-Gun Desire: Poems of the Erotic Left

Domingo 12 de septiembre,
1937 a las dos de la mañana: nací.
De ahí mis hábitos nocturnos
y el amor a los fines de semana.
Me clasificaron: ¿nena? rosadito.
Boté el rosa hace mucho tiempo
y escogí el color que más me gusta,
que son todos.
Me acompañan tres hijas y dos perros:
lo que me queda de dos matrimonios.
Estudié porque no había remedio;
afortunadamente lo he olvidado casi todo.

Tengo hígado, estómago, dos ovarios,
una matriz, corazón y cerebro, más accesorios.
Todo funciona en orden, por lo tanto,
río, grito, insulto, lloro y hago el amor.

Y después lo cuento.

Sunday 12 September, 1937
at 2 in the morning: I was born.
From there stem my nocturnal habits
and my love of weekends.
They classified me: small girl? pinkish.
I shed that hue long ago
and picked the colour I like best,
which is all of them.
3 daughters and 2 dogs come along with me:
what's left of 2 marriages.
I studied because what else;
luckily I've forgotten nearly everything.

I've got a liver, stomach, 2 ovaries,
a womb, heart and brain, plus accessories.
Everything works nicely and so
I laugh, yell insults, cry and make love.

And afterwards I recount it all.

Made of memories
        we are
of a blonde hair
a chest
        4 dead
        cigarettes
of rhythmical motions.

The rum sinks noisily into the throat
–10,000 dead cells –
and machine-gun
desire
in the fingers.

Strike a virgin pose.
> That's how they
> want us.

Softly, so softly
let's fornicate in our minds
with the skin of some kind of ghost.

> Feminine
> innocent
> we must smile.

And at night twist the knife
skip into the garden
abandon all this,
it reeks of death.

Let us wash our hair
and strip our bodies.

Sister, you and I
    have 2 breasts
    2 legs and a vulva.

We are not creatures
that live on air.

    No more smiles,
    no more false virgins already.

Nor martyrs waiting in bed
    for the male's odd droplet of drool.

You cleaned off the cum
and went in the shower.

      Swiped away the evidence
      but not the memory.

And now
    I'm here,
    frustrated without
    leave to be
    I ought to wait
and light the fire
and clean furniture
and slap butter on bread.

     With filthy banknotes
           you'll pay your fix,
           fle-e-ting.

And I cease to be human
    become old junk
      a little sick of all of this.

Sure,
I'm touchy, jealous,
changeable
and lustful.

What did you all expect?

Just that I'd have eyes,
glands,
brain, 33 years
and that I'd conduct myself
like the cypress in a cemetery?

They said a poem
should be less personal;
that you or me
are women's words.
That they aren't serious.

Luckily or unluckily
I carry on doing as I please.

Perhaps one day I'll employ
other means and go abstract.
Right now all I know
is that if one says something
it should be on a familiar theme.

All I am is sincere – and that's already plenty –
going on about my own joys and sorrows
I can tell of my love for strawberries,
                           for instance,
and my dislike for some people,
hypocrites, cruel, or just
for being stupid.
Or that I never asked to live
and dying doesn't draw me
except when I'm down.
That I'm made of words
above all.
That to be able to speak up
I make use of ink and paper in my own way.
I can't do anything about it.

However much I try
I won't write an essay
on set theory.

Maybe later on
I'll come across other ways to say things.
But right now
I don't care about that;
today I live here and this moment
and I am I
and I act as such.

For all the rest, alas I can't please everyone.
It's enough already I think to look to myself
and to try to accept me
with bones with muscles
with desires with sorrows.
And put my head through the door and watch the world
go by and say: "Good day. Here I am."
Even if you don't like it.
That's that.

New lover:
I want you to understand
that between your eyes
and my eyes
lies only desire.
That your white skin darkens at times
because he who marked me
is still here inside.

That I would like to say your name
                              and I can't
because I recall a different bed
other lips drinking from my breasts
when I open my mouth.

And when I cry
and I latch onto you with such force
it's not joy, lover.
It's memory.

You do well, great maestro.
I am the *guerrillera* in your regime,
            the ob-ject
that rises up with weapons of love
among your army of gorilla egotism
            and the power you imagine
at the end of your shift.

Track my steps
            in your soul
and quash well and without scruple
any shoot of subversive tenderness,
in case love catches
and your well-ordered dictatorship
            all goes to shit.

Perhaps I'll leave the struggle
to be a *guerrillera* leads to nothing
        but those things
you trace with so subtle a line.

I'm not going to wait for your next abuse
        nor for the day you chuck me
down the stairs
so the dogs can feed on my skull.

I know.
I'll never be anything more
than a *guerrillera* of love.
                I find myself somewhere
around there as on the erotic left.
Letting loose bullet after bullet
against the system.
Losing time and effort
preaching an outworn creed.

I'm going to end up
                left sprawled
                in the mountains
like that other zealot.

But since my struggle
isn't politics that counts for men
they'll never publish my diary
nor will photos of my face
– pop chic for the masses –
hang from walls
and decorate posters.

Revolutionary: tonight
I won't be in your bed.
Don't let love's subversion surprise you,
                    former proprietor.

You puff up your hide
and worry about social problems.
So much so you don't notice, impostor,
that at home in your manners
you mirror
just-so the best of tyrants.

Forrest Gander

How Not to Translate Mexican Poet Coral Bracho

I'll never forget reading a passage from Bruno Schulz's *Sanatorium Under the Sign of the Hourglass* in which the protagonist, a child named Joseph, is stalked and trapped against a hedgerow by a howling, vicious, black Alsatian dog that Joseph realizes, at the last second, is not a dog at all but, he explains in Celina Wieniewska's translation, just a "man, whom, by a simplifying metaphoric wholesale error, I had taken for a dog."[1]

Such dream logics are at work all through Coral Bracho's most personal and emotionally expressive collection of poems, *It Must Be a Misunderstanding* (New Directions, 2022), dedicated to her mother who died of complications from Alzheimer's. But instead of Schulz's characteristic atmosphere of anxiety and terror, Bracho finds tenderness, humor, grace, and even a kind of bravery in the interactions of personalities who encounter each other in a "Memory Care" facility which Bracho compares to a "kindergarten or asylum or abstract space." In the parallel worlds of the residents, a wall might be perceived as a man in a stiff suit, shadows might be taken for realities, light might be apprehended as traces of motion, quiet is strafed with fragments of voices, and everything exists and doesn't exist at the same time.

I chose to translate this whole book rather than another selected edition[2] of Bracho's more recent poems because, although composed of individual poems, *It Must Be a Misunderstanding* is really a deeply affecting book-length work whose force builds as the poems cycle through their sequences. The "plot" follows a general trajectory – from early to late Alzheimer's – with non-judgmental affection and compassionate watchfulness. We come to know an opinionated, demonstrative elderly woman whose resilience, in the face of her dehiscent memory, becomes most clear in her adaptive strategies. The poems involve us in the mind's

---

[1] Bruno Schulz, 'Sanatorium Under the Sign of the Hourglass', trans. Celina Wieniewska, *The New Yorker*, December 12, 1977, 44.
[2] *Firefly Under the Tongue: Selected Poems of Coral Bracho* (New York: New Directions, 2008), republished in the UK as part of *It Must be a Misunderstanding* (Manchester: Carcanet Press, 2022).

bafflement and wonder, in its creative quick-change adjustments, and in the emotional drama that draws us across the widening linguistic gaps that reroute communication.

Surely, one of the reasons that these poems speak so potently to me has to do with the fact of my own mother's recent death due to complications of Alzheimer's. A long section of my book *Be With* is concerned with my relationship with my mother during her last years. Now those poems are too painful for me to read, but I find Coral's poems uplifting – as I suspect you will.

It's typical in translations from Spanish to English that ambiguities derived from non-specific pronouns often need to be rendered more specifically. If in one line, a man and a woman are talking about a jaguar, for instance, and in the next line the poet writes "Tiene una mirada tranquila," the translator decides whether the man (he), the woman (she), or the jaguar (it) has that tranquil look. In poems that take place in a facility where people are literally losing their minds, mistaking identities, and experiencing hallucinations, the ambiguity of pronouns in Spanish can take on the legerdemainish drama of three-card monte. There's some guesswork involved.

Bracho's poems have philosophical and psychological underpinnings even when they are descriptive. Her work has always managed to mix abstraction and sensuality, but in this book the two merge into a particularly resonant combination. We are inside a mind, maybe many minds, considering a mystery with signal attentiveness, openness, and love.

To translate her poems badly, you could focus on the semantic meanings at the expense of sound, you could try to match the English syntax to the Spanish syntax, or you could keep yourself from "interpreting" because you insist on being objective – a stance akin to the one that vivisectionists took as they cut open living dogs without anesthesia and assured themselves that objectively, it was impossible to know for certain that the flinching, howling dog was really suffering in the way that humans suffer. To wit, the ground truth of my poetics of translation derives from the assumption that, like any act of reading, like any act of consciousness, translation is all about interpretation. How to weigh the meaning of sounds against semantic meanings? How to achieve a tone in a new language and culture that off-rhymes with the tone of the original? How to follow the original poem off the diving board into an expanding pool of readership with an arc and impact that, though they may be scored differently, might call to mind the grace, ferocity, humor – the personality – of the first dive? Importantly, I'm not interested in creating an archival document from a poem. Each book I translate requires new approaches. In my work with the Japanese poet Gozo Yoshimasu,[3] I include multiple translations and conversational notes that run expressively along the facing pages. There isn't a unified translational procedure that should satisfy anyone. Notably, Benjamin's provocative theories about translation aren't apparently at work in his own translations of Baudelaire's *Parisian Tableaux.*

To add some particularity: in a short poem from the same sequence of poems included with this statement, Coral Bracho writes:

(Diario)

> Vine por eso
> que pasó en Acteal.
> Eso espantoso que pasó. Sí,
> vine sola.
> Pero aquí están todos.
> Fue el gobierno, gritan.
> Y yo también.

Literally:

(Diary)

> I came for that
> that happened in Acteal.
> That horrid that happened. Yes,
> I came solo.
> But here are all of them.
> It was government, they shouted.
> And I also.

Remember that the speaker is likely a woman with Alzheimer's. She

---

[3] Yoshimasu Gozo, *Alice Iris Red Horse: Selected Poems of Yoshimasu Gozo, A Book in and on Translation,* ed. Forrest Gander (New York: New Directions, 2016).

remembers that she came somewhere in response to something that happened in Acteal. Anyone in Mexico can tell you what happened in Acteal. But few people north of the Mexican border remember that just before Christmas in 1997, at a prayer meeting in the tiny town of Acteal in Chiapas, forty-five Roman Catholic pacifists, including pregnant women and children, were massacred by a paramilitary unit on government orders. As the truth gradually came out, the by now former President of Mexico, Ernesto Zedillo, was granted "sovereign immunity" by the courts. I don't like the distraction of footnotes (unless they're used as a creative device). So I took a risk, regretting the loss of an empty adjective, "horrid," which modifies nothing but an implication in the original, but translating contextual information I felt essential to the thrust of the poem.

(Diary)

I came for that,
for what took place in Acteal, in Chiapas.
That horrific massacre. Yes,
I came alone.
But they're all here.
It was the government, they scream.
And I scream too.

Any translator can walk you through such decisions. Each is like the fulcrum of a see-saw on which the translation balances. But the translator's arguments, however copious and insistent, have little sway over how a reader reads and judges the translation. The brilliant arguments are all post mortem; the translation must be alive.

Coral Bracho

Translated from Spanish by Forrest Gander

It Must Be a Misunderstanding

(Observaciones)

Las piezas del rompecabezas
se pierden, pero no la mirada
que lo sabe suyo.
Las formas, los objetos, se funden,
se desmoronan; pero el sentido
del conjunto persiste: entre momentos,
entre ficciones,
bajo fracturas incesantes. Como un umbral,
un asidero.

(Observations)

The puzzle pieces
get lost but not the look
she knows to be hers.
The forms, the objects, they merge,
they crumble; but a feeling
for the ensemble remains: between moments,
between fictions,
despite constant fractures. Like a threshold,
a hand hold.

(Observations)

That bird,
dropping down to peck the asphalt
so close to her foot, is something
she's never encountered before.
There's nothing to compare it with;
nothing that links it to that cat,
nothing it shares
with that bush.
They're all unanticipated tenants;
convincing presences
in a space that, for the moment,
we share with them. There aren't kingdoms
that harbor them or separate them out
into their particular territories,
no words
that link them together. This thing here,
fluttering its wings now
and hopping between the grass and the dust,
it's unique.

(Alzheimer's. Follow-up)

Who is the President of this country?
– Well, it depends; for some
it's one person; for others it's someone else.
What is this called?
– I don't know, doctor, because I don't use
that; only you do.
How many children do you have?
– Quite a few.

What did you used to do?
– Now you're going to ask me
to draw a clock.
Did you like to dance?
– Yes, of course, of course I danced.
And did you ever travel?
– Yes, naturally.
Where to?
– Well, to the same place everyone went.

(Intuitions)

Which thread is the one that tells our story
and lends us substance
when there's no trajectory
by which to make sense of ourselves?
Which thread are we sure is vital?
The one that, maybe, ties together the handful of gestures
that comprise us; so we feel
we still have control. Gestures
that we repeat as certainties; that delineate
those certainties which once shaped us
and which now delimit
and nail us
to our shadows. Certainties
whose meaning and origin we don't know,
but which nevertheless enclose
and protect us, like dive helmets
or grilles;
which still let us to look through them
into the world:
that disquieting, incomprehensible
strangeness.

And let's see the red face of a jaguar that turns into a cat

1.

Show me something, I say to her.
And she shows me the red face of a jaguar
that turns into a cat. It has
such a calm, questioning look,
and everything around is yellow.
Now all that remains is that angle
of its ear cocked
to listen.

2.

There's a tree inside the flames.
But they aren't real flames, she explains.
Then she gets up and walks around. It's like the light
on a stage. And then she makes an adjustment.
To make it look like a forest, she tells us
from up there.

3.

Now it's a long-limbed ballerina
who leans over us.
She seems to be crying. But
her face pops off
because it's a white mask.
Get out of there, she demands. And they want
us to say OK. But no,
it's never clear, even when they tell us how.

4.

She's sitting at a table,
next to the kitchen. But it doesn't make sense.
As if what's happening
was just the same as any other day.
The same. But it can't be.
Even though the food is there.

5.

Give me. What?
And that's a little monkey. The hollows
in its face are just shadows.
Get out of there. And she pouts her lips as though
to give a kiss. She comes nearer
to plant her kiss. But she doesn't do it.
She blows the kiss from a distance.

6.

As if she were looking at herself
planting a kiss. There's someone who goes off in a boat.
He clings to the mast with both arms. Like a
flag. And suddenly it's no longer him
but a fish that goes off in the boat
as it sets out. A sailing ship.

7.

But already that ship points upward
and it's flying. I don't understand any of this, I tell her.
It's all pure silliness.
And there's an image, but it seems
shrouded by a mist
that's terribly dense, terribly dark.

8.

The launch that leaves now
is tiny and very fast.
It pivots and spins in the air.
The man at its wheel wears a sombrero
and leaps around like a dancer.
He's leaping, scratching lines into the sky.

9.

But why don't you tell me something, I say to her.
And she shows me some little notebooks
that speak. Pay attention
to what they tell you, someone tells me
who has just entered through another door.

(She speaks)

I don't want that woman ever
to come back,
she spouts nothing but nonsense:
Now lift your arms, now move your foot. Nothing
but nonsense. Why should I do
whatever she wants?
I got really mad.
I pushed her. Get out of here, get out,
I told her.
Then I shut the door.

(Intuitions)

Meaning is what accommodates things
wherever they feel
they can be.
It judges how far they go
and how near they come
or how they converge.
There's a calm, a serene joy,
that things peel open and render
if meaning touches them.
When it's part
of the things we create,
when it rushes side by side with them, or lights them up:
that's its breath
its force.

(Diary)

You're a bunch of thieves
and you know it too – she shouted
in the hospital,
waking up from the operation without her thin bracelet
of little crystals.

There's no rush to pay – said the doctor
a moment later –,
it doesn't have to be now.

The last thing that holds you up
against the collapse of memory,
the last thing that breaks and unspools her,
is the search
for meaning; to recognize yourself,
and your avid, intimate alliance
with the species;
to apprehend and imagine what another feels; to follow the intonations
of language; to name
and conceive of abstractions: love,
injustice; and still to enjoy the beauty,
the music.

Johannes Göransson

The Metamorphic Sublime:
On Translating Eva Kristina Olsson

I.

Eva Kristina Olsson has a long and rich bibliography that includes books of poetry, plays, performances and films. She emerged in the late 80s and early 90s as part of a new wave of women poets – which also included Ann Jäderlund and Katarina Frostensson – who wrote strange, elliptical, and mysterious, but at the same time forceful and often erotic, poetry. But Olsson always had an ambivalent relationship to the literary establishment. Although her first book, *The Crime* (1988), was published by the biggest Swedish publisher, Albert Bonnier, she was at the same time affiliated with Stockholm Surrealist Group, a transgressive and antisocial group engaged in Surrealist experiments, and acted-out performance pieces, often as street theater. Throughout her career she has veered between success and outsiderness. She has published with a number of presses, big and small, and her performances have tended to eschew the established venues. What all these works – which could be said to form a kind of unwieldy, mutating total artwork – have in common is a combination of the broken down (body, words) held together by a luminous intensity.

To some extent, Olsson achieved a critical breakthrough of sorts with her 2018 book *The Angelgreen Sacrament* (Black Square Editions, 2021), an intense, occult book about the interactions between the poet and one (or several) angels. "Interactions" is too bland a word for the intensive relationship with these entities, but it is not always easy to determine how they are interacting – what they are doing to each other:

in a nothing vibrating nothing

an angel without wings

but with wings

and with wings

creates the white endlessly nothing soft rose petals

my pistachiogreen wings

of your endlessly fragile glance

in the allthetime collapsing hair

you rise

It is not clear who is saying or doing what to whom. Is the speaker the angel or the human meeting the angel? Are they even different? Is it the reader who is being addressed by an angel? And at the same time as the poem is full of "nothing," it is profoundly erotic and physical: the "nothing" vibrates "pistachiogreen wings," the nothing is a "Nothing soft rose petals" – a nothing that is also physical, natural, beautiful, present.

The "allthetime" repetend in this section emblematizes the intensity of the encounter. In Swedish, the phrase "i det hela tiden" suggest an ongoinginess, but the more conventional translation "constantly" is too abstract, so we created the neologism "allthetime," making sure that it contained the word "hela" ("all") to bring in the complete, overwhelming quality of the interaction. The experience is all-encompassing in both time and space; we are submerged in it even though it is made up of "nothing." In an interview Olsson says about the encounter in the book: "It is the ultimate living thing for me to talk to."

Another way of putting it might be to say that the poem is the "ultimate living" experience. Roberto Calasso has written: "Whatever else it might be, the divine is certainly the thing that imposes with maximum intensity the sensation of being alive. This is the immediate: but pure intensity, as a continuous experience, is "impossible," overwhelming."[4]

---

[4] Roberto Calasso, *Literature and the Gods* (New York: Vintage, 2002), 39.

It is this kind of "divine" experience Olsson both discusses and involves the reader in: it is almost too much. The result is what Calasso has called "absolute literature": "literature at its most piercing, its most intolerant of any social trappings."[5] Olsson's book is the best instance I know of "absolute literature." Reader, speaker, angel: all are constantly pierced through by the luminous and intense encounter. At times the encounter may seem erotic but it is also violent. This may be why the poem has to constantly reassure the angel, the human – perhaps most of all the reader – not to be "afraid" but to go further into the poem, the encounter. This may be why Aase Berg, in a review, called the book "tortuously beautiful".[6]

The piercingness is represented – or manifested – by a green light, a light that figures as a motif in the text as well as in the layout of the book – which is covered by a shimmering blue-green, semi-translucent cover as well as several pages that are simply green without text, as if the text had been obliterated by an eruption of "pistachiogreen." This green color seems both spiritual and physical. I am reminded of Michael Taussig's discussion of sacred color that can transform the viewer: "Color vision becomes less a retinal and more a total bodily activity to the fairytale extent that in looking at something, we may even pass into the image."[7] And: "color comes across here as more a presence than a sign, more a force than a code, and more as *calor,* which is why, so I believe, John Ruskin declared in his book *Modern Painters* that 'colour is the most sacred element of all visible things'."[8]

Olsson's model of the "sacred" is notably different than the Christian model. Rather than Augustine's model of the soul as something pure inside of a sinful body, of interiority as purity, Olsson's sacred is in unstable, mutating surfaces. She focuses on the body – of the speaker and the angel – as it "vibrates" and "collapses." In the interview mentioned

---

[5] "An Interview with Eva Kristina Olsson by Johannes Göransson" 20 August 2020, https://actionbooks.org/2020/08/an-interview-with-eva-kristina-olsson-by-johannes-goransson/ Accessed 28 August 2022.

[6] Aase Berg, "Eva Kristina Olsson's *Det ängelsgröna sakramentet*", https://actionbooks.org/2020/07/torturously-beautiful-aase-berg-reviews-eva-kristina-olssons-the-angelgreen-sacrament/ Accessed 28 August 2022.

[7] Michael Taussig, "What Colour is the Sacred?" https://press.uchicago.edu/Misc/Chicago/790060.html Accessed 28 August 2022.

[8] Michael Taussig, "What Colour is the Sacred?"

above, Olsson mentions that there is a secondary subject matter – or "inspiration" – to the book: "a long pistachio-green prom dress I wore when I was 16, 17 years old." The intensity of the "pistachio green" color brings together the body of the angel and a dress she wore when she was young, the sacred and the profane existing as part of the same fabric.

2.

It's a convention that translators writing about their translations should focus on the "challenges" and "difficulties." This accomplishes a number of things. To begin with, it shows just how skilled the translator is to understand the texts and their contexts. Perhaps more importantly, it shows that the translation is indeed, as US conventions have had it for a long time, "impossible." Or in more scholarly terms, it points out the difference between cultures. This "estrangement" creates distance. In leading scholar Lawrence Venuti's work, such estrangement – which he calls for translators to emphasize with "foreignizing" translation modes – is a necessary reminder to the English-language reader that the book is in translation, that there is cultural difference. The translation becomes, in other words, pedagogical.[9]

I was never convinced of these arguments. They seem fundamentally anti-poetry to me. Reek of what Rita Felski calls "the hermeneutics of suspicion," the mode of critical writing that always holds the poem at a "critical distance."[10] It's a stance that emphasizes expertise and mastery, of the critic being in control of the text. If we are going to see the translation as an act of mimesis, I would prefer to think of mimesis more along the lines of how Taussig, drawing on Walter Benjamin's essay "The Mimetic Faculty," describes it as a kind of sympathetic magic that creates transformation: "…mimesis has an inbuilt propensity to provoke a chain reaction in which things become other things in a process of mimetic fission… This I call the 'metamorphic sublime.'"[11] According to Taussig, this "mimetic excess"

---

[9] Lawrence Venuti, *The Translator's Invisibility* (New York: Routledge, 1995).
[10] Rita Felski, "Context Stinks!" *New Literary History* 42, No. 4 (2011), 573–591.
[11] Michael Taussig, *Mastery of Non-Mastery in the Age of Meltdown* (Chicago: University of Chicago Press, 2020), 40.

runs counter to the ideal of mastery by provoking a sense of childlike "re-enchantment." Like with the color, Taussig's (and Benjamin's) mimesis is volatile, capable not just of helping a subject make sense of experience, but of pulling the subject in, transforming them.

In translating Eva Kristina Olsson's *The Angelgreen Sacrament*, there are plenty of difficulties and challenges. The language is complex – full of seeming errors and distortions – such as when objects seem to lose subjects, when plurals and singulars mingle, or when suddenly a capital letter shoots up in the middle of a word. But for me none of those difficulties are impediments or distancing. Rather they involve me – as a reader, as a translator – in a relationship that could be called "the metamorphic sublime." As the translator, I become the poet, and I become the angel. I become green with luminosity.

Eva Kristina Olsson

Translated from Swedish by Johannes Göransson

From *The Angelgreen Sacrament*

the hair
my green hair that throngs
but lets in
the black flecks
the round ones
the ones wholly without other names
and how they throng
wholly beyond my hair
the orange circles in the white
nothing
only a sideglance in your
nothing only my green steps
when you go
and collapse
Nothing is everything
you are afraid
don't be afraid
I am the only
I am the only
one you see
sitting on the step,
angel mounted in the stone step :

you, then

in the cooly vibrating

expanding vibrating nothing

the step

one step

then and now this mounted fear

in fear

this nothing in the step

which encloses itself in hair

which opens itself in hair

and flies in the white endless

nothing soft rose petals

don't be afraid

you are afraid

I am afraid

my pistachiogreen back glows through my endlessly fragile wings

this hair of orange circles

can you see her back in those of nothing

other than orange circles

I see, I fasten my eyes

my pistachiogreen back illuminates my endlessly fragile wings

my pistachiogreen back illuminates the orange circles

in a nothing vibrating nothing

an angel without wings

but with wings

and with wings

creates the white endlessly nothing soft rose petals

my pistachiogreen wings

of your endlessly fragile glance

in the allthetime collapsing hair

you rise

in the allthetime collapsing back

you rise

in the allthetime cool

you rise

in the allthetime vibrating

you rise

in the allthetime expanding

you rise

in the allthetime nothing

you rise

in the allthetime collapsing angel-me

and reach your arms

toward no one's arms no one's hands

only this nothing which loves you

and wants you close

which you want to be near

You are afraid

be afraid

see that longing

go to that longing which lies on the third step : your sacrament :

Katherine M. Hedeen

"in the crevices of being... in the sinuous sea reflection...": On Translating the muskrat notebook *by Víctor Rodríguez Núñez*

Translation, when tolerated, is travel. The question is always: WHERE? It is often a demand: WHERE!

What to do, then, with a book by a Cuban poet entitled *the muskrat notebook? el cuaderno de la rata almizclera / the muskrat notebook* is a book-length poem by Víctor Rodríguez Núñez (Havana, 1955).[1] It belongs to Rodríguez Núñez's most recent poetic cycle, a chronicling of the poet's unique migratory experience that foregrounds a profound questioning of nationalism and cultural identity. Its fluid poetic subject proposes movement, edgelessness; rejects "at-home-ness":[2] a conscious choice to be in many places at once. It is very much about: WHERE. And yet: WHERE is Cuba? Here there are no maracas, cigars, rums, bearded rebels in army fatigues, picturesque poverty, leftover socialist nostalgia, tropic temptation. *the muskrat notebook* is decidedly not the Cuba demanded. My translation work mirrors the place/space fluidity of this poetry. It is a conscious choice about WHERE.

**

the stone condition in the swelling…
in the crevices of being

***

My approach to translating Spanish American poetry places *place* at its center. It follows the call of another Cuban poet, the nineteenth-century writer and patriot José Martí, to respond to US neo-colonialist aggression strategically, precisely from *place*; in his case, from the other América: "Our América." Martí's decolonizing move is to choose

---

[1] In 2017 it was published in Argentina by Buenos Aires Poetry and in 2018 in Spain with La Garúa.

[2] Pierre Joris's term in *A Nomad Poetics*. (Middletown CT: Wesleyan University Press, 2003), 26.

WHERE. It is my countermap.

Such charting is a response to two main trends in the US with regard to Spanish American poetry in English translation. The first began in the sixties, when poets like Robert Bly, W.S. Merwin, and James Wright, among others, translated and published Spanish-language poets in a reaction to what they thought to be a stale, conventional, formalist poetry in the US, bereft of emotion and political commitment (the Cuban Revolution, which triumphed in 1959, also played a role in turning eyes toward the region).[3]

Perhaps the poet who best exemplifies this trend is the Chilean Nobel Prize Winner Pablo Neruda. While areas of his work are undoubtedly avant-garde, much of what he is known for in English translation is a kind of innate connection to sensuality, passion, feeling, emotion, and the body, which those from the "modern" North have lost and are thus drawn to: a more "primitive," "passionate" art. Bly referred to such poetry as "hot Surrealism." Even the Spanish poet Federico García Lorca described it as "a light that is full, romantic, cruel, excessive, mysterious, American."[4] Likewise, Neruda's political commitment (and that of poets writing in Spanish more generally) has been over-emphasized in simplistic and obvious ways, hailed as a poetry of witness.

This shaping of the canon (for lack of a better word) of Spanish-language poetry in English translation highlights work that is not necessarily complex, cerebral, or intellectual. The North/South dichotomy is typical of neo/colonialist discourse: the South is sensual and irrational, an exotic land of corruption, dictators, and guerrillas; the North is cerebral and theoretical, a land of democracy and freedom, and more specifically, freedom of expression. Indeed, the erasure of Spanish as intellectual and difficult mimics the general trend in the US of considering Spanish a "practical" and "easier" language when compared to traditionally "harder" languages, like French or German.

The second (and more recent) trend would seem to offset the one described above. Independent US poetry presses over the past fifteen years have sought out Spanish American poets who fall under the umbrella term of marginalized voices, in a move that echoes the very popular

---

[3] See Jonathan Mayhew's *Apocryphal Lorca: Translation, Parody, Kitsch* (Chicago: University of Chicago Press, 2009) for an excellent discussion of all this.

[4] García Lorca introducing Pablo Neruda at the University of Madrid on December 6, 1934. https://letralia.com/234/articulo03.htm Accessed 17 October 2022.

and successful trend in the US of poetry based on identity politics. In their search to discover the underrepresented, small presses end up proposing just as limiting a canon (albeit different), handpicking poets who, in terms of content, often conveniently mirror back to a woke US readership their own concerns and anxieties about representation, and, in terms of form, either privilege a direct, conversational tone, easily consumable (and translatable) or a so-called experimental aesthetic, also based on a mirroring back of US-based definitions of what formal experimentation entails.

What unsettles in either case is the question of place. WHERE? The impetus of such endeavors is what we, positioned in the US, can "get out" of Spanish American poetry. It serves *US*, whether it be a reaction to domestic literary trends or as a way to brand a certain kind of poetry wokeness. The cultural superiority – and the unidirectionality – behind such curation goes unchecked by a literary establishment that is fiercely English-only and firmly rooted in the discourse and practice of policing citizenship.

Martí's call to countermap means intentionally choosing to translate poets whose work falls both outside the confines of what a US reader might think a poet in Spanish "should" write like, as well as what Spanish American poetic canons have established as representative for their own readership. It is at once a response to a unidirectional, US-centric circulation of ideas and a challenging of the Spanish American poetry canon itself. This is where I place Rodríguez Núñez: he doesn't write the way a Cuban should write, on either side of the Florida Strait.

****

in the sinuous sea reflection...
just certain nervations endure

*****

WHERE? In *el cuaderno de la rata almizclera* place is in the Agabama River's swelling; the subtle nod to the 10-line décima – the quintessential form of Cuban popular verse and nineteenth-century nation-building; the muskrat itself: the poetic voice's endless search for identity and identification beyond the limitations of the commonplace. WHERE? In *the muskrat notebook*, place is in the opting for disruption and detour.

Víctor Rodríguez Núñez

Translated from Spanish by Katherine M. Hedeen

el cuaderno de la rata almizclera

5

para Jean Portante

con su carbón la rata
                puede atizar el brillo
y apagar la mudez
imagen en astillas
mensaje que fluye a contracorriente
con su cisco la rata
ante el viento en jirones hielo crudo
lunas que no desisten
la nada se da vuelta
                forma comprometida

¿y la gracia almizclada
en los soles que no pudieron ser?
¿cuando el hielo devela
la nerviosa osamenta de las cosas?
¿vigilaba latente
a recaudo de toda condición?
¿cuando el torrente cuaja
al pie de la impureza de los sauces?
¿agitaba en el sueño sumergido
las ondas del estar?

the muskrat notebook

5

for Jean Portante

with its coal the rat
                    can stir up the glow
and put out the muteness
image in splinters
message flowing crosscurrent
with its culm the rat
before the wind in shreds raw ice
moons not giving up
the nothingness turns upside down
                              committed form

what about the musky grace
in the suns helpless to be?
when the ice reveals
the nervous bony structure of things?
did it keep watch
safe and sound from any condition?
when the torrent curdles
at the foot of willow impurity?
in the underwater dream did it shake
the waves of staying?

14

making the rounds the angles
                                that don't overlap
will the thirst the hail
its eager sand clear up?
another décima in germ
cuban grassquit frightening a condor?
snowtrack like shelter
for the hostile light?
before the interception
                        to faithfully abandon

arriving from death
with a new form in hand
in frozen tremble
water lilies at right angles in the swelling
amber silences
                        accented oversights
breasts in flight from the mist
beneath fingernails
                        loyal urine
stains of inspiration

19

the rain works sidewalks
                                germinating pebbles
raise the never aromas
you growl at the rain
                        dorian mode
you wave your red and white tail at it

mark off its sleeplessness
the rain has cracked lips
puddles for bravery
                    soul not incarnate

it rains the whole decimal night
no torment drop
in the muddy air
                    the ray is a larva
the rhythm dries up squares
overshadows the swelling once and for all
sand in hand
                    in the reluctant dawn
anchored to its smiling silence
you don't stop croaking

21

if you dekernel the sky
                        its artificiality
the oriole nest in the living room
the wine with hive
along with the thirst you drink from its mouth
the color magenta remains
                            edgeless in charcoal
the rafter in the eye of the whirlwind
the stone condition in the swelling
your essence fermented

if you call up the pollen
                        that interweaves the fury

the moon on the cliff
rusty in the waiting from the vertigo
you shouldn't fear a thing
                              because the saltpeter illuminates
the whitecaps converge
to a rhythm with sense with memory
in the crevices of being
your appearance stagnates like a lotus

23

red dead you wait for
                              it to be time to crossbreed
the penumbra drips with sand
and its mathematical honey
insomnia supply
at its lowest level like crude oil
the out-of-the-way waters
pouring from the bitten lip
desire slits
                night throwing sparks

the dilemma comes with the dawn
and drains your sleep
life is like an oregon river
it ends in foam
                in the sudden pond
the wind corolla musks
the sphincters open
leaps of spawning crosscurrent
rain is the proof
the sky needs mending

27

to a pulp the light
                it doesn't complain
but it does leave you blind
to twist the arm of bold reflection
perched like a swarm
to break the rib of
the void's gleam
                its queenless hovering
the violence runs back
the pupils hidden in the honey

you're cloaked by the vision
                        not harvested blinking
your existing is not shaped
from the knot that resembles the foliage weave
your being is not shaped
from the board sanded down by countless downpours
barely the keyhole owl eye
to look inside so nothing was left outside
an image in heat
                fertilized by the void

33

to read from your lips
in the sinuous sea reflection
the signal not agreed upon
                        let the willow get red
later to hear the interior prayer
without the deflowered Buddha shorn

then to reject becoming known
in cayama's black seagull
and to reach an agreement
on the very edge of a caesura

the dreams on the coast
slip through your fingers like harpoons
nobody ought to hone them
                         on the foamy grinding stone
their wounds can fester
if the moon if the celestial saltpeter
                                 stick to them
muteness forgetfulness ooze
see-through bleeding as it dries utters
your plea in the tide

34

no one gets upset anymore about the swellings
the laying waste of nests
                          the avant-garde prayer
of the agabama bursting its banks
the discourse cast its dams
one can flow
with equanimity with clarity
the water hyacinth and you conspired
so the agabama might once more be
thorny dialectic

even the tungsten can sometimes overflow
reluctant to be ring
                     existence swelling

with its cows bloated from thirst
with its impatient lotus flowers
you jump to the mercurial current
you don't have a flat tail you swim out of tune
better never than late
your mother on the far side
                                    won't let you cross

41

rustic spelling
                    phonetics wave
like a red triangle
the hawk pounces
                        with its talons in h
the gerunds water at the shoreless c
with their silky horns
                              the mist makes a k
this copies the stump
waves crystallized in cursive

morning with swelling
                            and clouds in bulk
the river overflows memory
and takes everything with it
its gold still unsettled
the lily pile
next to the cow gravely keeled over
the rat actually misunderstood
its accented strokes
                      in your fatal longhand

43

the book of political fables
like a cedar in autumn
has lost its proletariat leaves
just certain nervations endure
and a few branches
                    rustling time
those greens still faithful to the trunk
to bitter optimism
disciplined they turn over their beauty
honor's relic

nature gets political
atoms are southpaws
                    shift to red
and cells search for a better world
like the rat
            you live where others die
gnaw on dams and genetically modified corn
from root to lightning bolt
the sprig on the anvil
                    even if god doesn't believe it

Meena Kandasamy

Translation as Circuit-breaking: Towards a Feminist Rendering of the Tamil Classic Thirukkural

Tamil is one of the oldest languages of the world according to linguistic historians, first making its appearance around 2500 BCE. Spoken by about 78 million people in the south Indian state of Tamil Nadu, in Tamil Eelam, and elsewhere around the world, it is the world's oldest surviving language too. Modern linguistic scholarship places the oldest extant Tamil literature, at around 300 BCE. *Thirukkural* holds a special place in Tamil literature, and is often seen by everyone – from poets to politicians – as reflective of the Tamil philosophy of life. Scholars have variously placed it between 31 BCE and 400 CE. It was authored by Thiruvalluvar, and while biographical details of the poet have been lost to history, the text remains vital, a heartbeat to Tamil culture and imagination.

The 1,330 verses of *Thirukkural* are divided between three sections (*Aram, Porul, Inbam* denoting Virtue, Wealth and Desire respectively). They are written in the *kural venba,* an ancient metrical form dating to the Sangam era and one of the most difficult stanzaic structures of Tamil prosody. The first line consists of four feet (*cīr,* in Tamil), and the second of three. The *Inbaththuppaal,* or *Kamaththuppaal* excerpts from which are translated here, consists of 250 kurals divided into twenty-five chapters.

The first translation of the Thirukkural in English appeared more than 220 years ago, in 1794. In these intervening years, more than one hundred translations have appeared in English. So far, only one of these translators was a woman. In the hands of its multiple commentators, colonial translators, missionaries, Hindu reformists and erudite Tamil male scholars, the love poetry of the Thirukkural came to be de-eroticised and almost sanitised to suit Victorian social mores or didactic perversions.

For me, the first feminist decision was to translate the *Kamath-thuppaal* as a standalone text. When the Italian Jesuit priest Constantine Joseph Beschi (who adopted the Tamil name Veeramamunivar) translated the *Thirukkural* into Latin in the seventeenth century, he only worked on the first two sections of the kural – the section dealing with virtue, and that dealing with statecraft/governance. The third section, on love, was seen as too taboo for a Jesuit priest. Although Veeramamunivar's work enabled European scholars of the time to learn of the greatness of Tamil scholarship, his self-censorship marked the beginning of a gradual neglect towards this portion of the *Thirukkural*.

My translation progressed in much the same manner that Tamil commentators of the *Thirukkural* approached the work – first through the semantic breakdown of the component words in order to explain its meaning. This is termed as *padha urai* in Tamil, and goes back to the times of the earliest commentators. This was a politically charged exercise because even at the earliest level of commentary, words are already extrapolated and filled up with regressive/patriarchal meanings/interpretations. For instance, in a kural (1241), Parimelazhagar, the most authoritative commentator (13th century), adds that the woman is "losing shame which is dearer than life." This is shocking because nowhere does Thiruvalluvar write that shame is dearer than life. This is how there has been an imposition and infiltration of patriarchal notions into the text. For me, undertaking a feminist translation was to break free from this hegemonic tradition.

Before I embarked on my own rendering, I took the time to pause and to observe how judgmental values of reserve, Victorian morality, and rigid Tamil notions of masculine-feminine value-systems have impregnated the translations. This was an essential step, like a circuit-breaker, to ensure that these do not get carried over into my translation even subconsciously, or as a result of deep-rooted conditioning.

Likewise, I also worked towards eliminating archaic words from translations. Often, because the men who were translating the kural happened to be Christian missionaries or Hindu religious reformists, there is a marked tendency of the translated text to be discreet and vague. There are many instances where sex is referred as union or congress in the English translation. Sulking and quarrelling go by the word *bouderie*, which, for all the French affectation, is not easily accessible to the reader in English.

Often, the *Thirukkural* has been translated as a long, one-sentence translation into English, or has been rendered as a rhyming couplet.

English has the word order of Subject-Verb-Object (SVO), whereas Tamil has the word order of Subject-Object-Verb. The main verb of a Tamil couplet or kural comes at the end of it, whereas in English it comes in the middle. This affects the translation because for poetry, the minute of revealing the twist, the turn of thought, the moment of comparison is very crucial. To remain true to the spirit of the original rather than the visual form, I used a four-line stanza to capture the two-line kural because the line-breaks helped me achieve the dénouements which existed in the first and second halves of the kural. I think remaining true to the mood of the kural was important to me as a feminist – especially because a lot of the verses express female desire, and it was important to capture how it was expressed.

Weeding out patriarchal translations was important. I can provide a multitude of examples from within the text of my translation, but for the purposes of this essay on feminist translation, let me choose the easy, but contentious word *nirai* (நிறை). The University of Madras Tamil Lexicon, lists out the meaning of this word in this manner:

நிறை³ niṟai , *n.* < நிறை¹-. 1. [K. *neṟe*.] Completion, completeness; பூர்த்தி. நிறைப் பெருஞ் செல்வத்து நின்றக்கடைத்தும் (நாலடி, 360). 2. Fulness, repletion, copiousness, one of eight *pāṭar-payaṉ*, q. v.; எண்வகைப் பாடற்பயன்களுள் ஒன்று. (சிலப். 3, 16, உரை.) 3. Excellence, splendour; மாட்சிமை. வானவரதேத்து நிறை கழலோன் (திருவாச. 13, 13). (சூடா.) 4. (Mus.) Note repeated often in singing a musical piece; அடுத்தடுத்துவரும் ஸ்வரம். 5. (Mus.) A time-measure consisting of two beats; இரண்டு தாக்குடைய தாளவகை. (பரிபா. 17, 18.) 6. Large water-pot; நீர்ச்சால். (சூடா.)7. The ceremony of filling up a pot with *nāṭ-katir* and paddy; நாட்கதிரும் நெல்லும் ஒரு பானையிலிட்டு நிறைக்கும் விசேடம். *Nāñ.* 8. Desire; ஆசை. (அக. நி.)

This word occurs in half a dozen instances, and most often it has been rendered by male translators as 'chastity.' Let us take the example of kural 1251 where this word (நிறை) occurs. Chastity is not what the original text uses, and to use it there is an imposition of post-dated cultural values on a classical text.

As a poet, translator, woman, and feminist, I want to avoid the burden of regressive ideas foisted on a text that actually burns with longing, that only ever fusses about with shame in order to speak of the shame itself. So, when it was my turn to translate this kural, I chose "unwavering mind", a choice that I justify also because *nirai* means that fullness, strength, containment. I wanted to bring the quality of something that is self-fulfilled and doesn't have to wander or waver because it also speaks against society's easy lazy patriarchal internalization: that women have fickle minds. I have rendered the kural 1251 in this manner:

> The battle-axe of passion
> breaks down the door
> of my unwavering mind,
> bolted with my coyness.

In my bid to create a feminist translation, I also decided to avoid the words husband and wife in the very few instances where they occur in the text, to stop burdening that text of love with a social custom whose contemporary connotations may be far removed from how they were employed in Thiruvalluvar's time. I have used the word man, or lover, or woman or lover. I think this sort of feminist translation of a classical text is a necessary intervention to course-correct what has been happening with the *Thirukkural* for the past several centuries.

Thiruvalluvar

Translated from Tamil by Meena Kandasamy

Berating Her Heart

1291. அவர்நெஞ்சு அவர்க்காதல் கண்டூம்
எவன்நெஞ்சே நீஎமக்கு ஆகா தது.

Having seen how his heart
goes along with him, dear heart,
whose are you, when you
don't get along with me?

1292. உறாஅ தவர்க்கண்ட கண்ணும் அவரைச்
சுறாஅரனெச் சுறேியனெ நெஞ்சு.

Having seen he cannot
come close or commit,
my heart takes no offence,
it still goes in search of him.

1293. கெட்டார்க்கு நட்டார்இல் என்பதோ நெஞ்சநீ
பெட்டாங்கு அவர்பின் சுலெல்.

It is said – 'The ruined have
no friends' – Is what why,
my heart, you abandon me
and run after him?

1294. இனிஅன்ன நின்னொடு சூழ்வார்யார்
நெஞ்சே துனிசெய்து தூவ்வாய்காண் மற்று.

First, sulk and refuse; then,
yield and enjoy – you failed
to follow this – who will now
rally around you, my heart?

1295. பெறாஅமை அஞ்சும் பெறின்பிரிவு
அஞ்சும் அறாஅ இடும்பைத்தென் நெஞ்சு.

The fear of not attaining my lover
and, after having him, the fear
of separation – my heart lives
in this perpetual agony.

1296. தனியே இருந்து நினைத்தக்கால் என்னைத்
தினிய இருந்ததென் நெஞ்சு.

Alone, I remained
thinking of him
as my heart kept
at devouring me.

1297. நாணும் மறந்தேன் அவர்மறக் கல்லாளென்
மாணா மடநெஞ்சிற் பட்டு.

Under the influence
of my shameless, foolish heart,
I forgot all bashfulness but
I could not forget him.

1298. எள்ளின் இளிவாம்என்று எண்ணி அவர்திறம்
உள்ளம் உயிர்க்காதல் நெஞ்சு.

Caught in the love of its life,
my heart recollects his greatness alone
because blaming him brings
disgrace upon it.

1299. துன்பத்திற்கு யாரே துணையாவார்
தாமுடைய நெஞ்சந் துணையல் வழி.

Who, whoever will be,
my companion-in-grief,
when mine own heart
refuses to stay with me?

1300. தஞ்சம் தமரல்லர் ஏதிலார் தாமுடைய
நெஞ்சம் தமரல் வழி.

My own heart is not my ally.
Will strangers send
their own heart
my way?

The Delights of Sulking

1321. இல்லை தவறவர்க்கு ஆயினும் ஊடுதல்
வல்லது அவர்அளிக்கு மாறு.

No, no, he has no faults,
but my sullenness has such strength,
you see – it makes him pay back
with much more, much more love

1322. ஊடலின் தோன்றும் சிறுதுனி நல்லளி
வாடினும் பாடு பெறும்.

In a lover's quarrel,
a little anger does arise –
but it does good, it makes
a fading love bloom afresh.

1323. புலத்தலின் புத்தேள்நாடு உண்டோ
நிலத்தொடு நீரியை தன்னார் அகத்து.

Is there any celestial world
greater than those of lovers
faking displeasure, their hearts
made for each other, like earth and rain?

1324. புல்லி விடாஅப் புலவியுள் தோன்றுமென்
உள்ளம் உடைக்கும் படை.

The lover's quarrel,
leading to a ceaseless
embrace, is the army
that smashes my heart.

1325. தவறிலர் ஆயினும் தாம்வீழ்வார் மென்றோள்
அகறலின் ஆங்கொன் றூடைத்து.

Though he be faultless,
there is something about
swiftly tearing away from
our lover's soft shoulders.

1326. உணலினும் உண்டது அறல்இனிது காமம்
புணர்தலின் ஊடல் இனிது.

Lovers' quarrels are sweeter
than love-making itself,
finishing a meal sweeter
than the feast itself.

1327. ஊடலில் தோற்றவர் வென்றார் அதுமன்னும்
கூடலிற் காணப் படும்.

In a lovers' quarrel,
the loser wins – and
this truth is seen
in the sex.

1328. ஊடிப் பெறுகுவம் கொல்லோ
நுதல்வெயர்ப்பக் கூடலில் தோன்றிய உப்பூ.

Will sulking make us
make love – the way sex
makes our foreheads
sweat salt?

1329. ஊடுக மன்னோ ஒளியிழை யாமிரப்ப
நீடுக மன்னோ இரா.

My shimmering beloved,
keep on pouting –
dear night, stay endless
as I plead with her!

1330. ஊடுதல் காமத்திற்கு இன்பம் அதற்கின்பம்
கூடி முயங்கப் பெறின்.

Sex takes delight
in sulking, which
delights in
getting sex.

Ghazal Mosadeq

Defeat as Resistance in the Poetry of Mehdi Akhavan Saless

A leading Modernist poet Mehdi Akhavan Saless (1928, Mashhad–1990, Tehran), published under the pseudonym M. Omid. Akhavan based his poetic practice on resistance to imperialist influences and on domestic injustice within his country. His methods of opposing those powers were quite unusual within the Iranian tradition during and after the constitutional revolution (1905–1911). Akhavan's fragmented narrative style is based on strong allegorical principles, working through archaic as well as contemporary metaphors. The modest and self-deprecating tone of his verse does not call for unification in the face of the enemy. Rather, it criticises the domestic and foreign sources that he holds responsible for the overwhelming sense of political despair present in his country.

Akhavan's linguistically and syntactically elaborate work is imbued with historical references that evokes the literary and political history of Iran. This creates difficulties in translating his poetry, especially to English, with which it shares so little cultural space. Yet, meditating on his work, even if we lose some of his poetic subtleties in the process of translation, the destruction itself, I argue, is very much the essence of Akhavan's intention within the realm of poetry. He is known as the "poet of defeat."[1] His writing hints time and again at being silenced and betrayed by the *self* and the *other*.

He writes, "we are the conquerors of the cities long gone… we are the heirs of the sad purity of the epochs… we are narrators of forgotten tales…".[2] His pseudonym, Omid (which means "hope") is meant ironically, since hope is what he lacks. In another poem he writes, "they wonder, Omid? and so hopeless? / [that is because] I am the elegist of my dead country.'[3] Akhavan is buried beside Ferdowsi in the city of Tous.

---

[1] Abd al-Alī Dastgheib. Shāer-e Shekast (Tehrān: Intishārāt-i Murvārīd, 1994), p. 93

[2] Mehdī Akhavān Sāleth. *Ākhar-i Shāhnāmah: majmūah-i shir* (Tehrān: Enteshārāt-e Morvārīd, 1994), p. 44

[3] Mehdī Akhavān Sāleth. *Torā ey kohan būm o bar dūst dāram: majmūah-i shir* (Tehrān: Enteshārāt-e Morvārīd, 1992) p. 99

Akhavan's major artistic preoccupation was the Iranian coup of 1953, after which he was incarcerated twice. *Zemestān* (1956), the first collection Akhavan published after the coup, revealed not only the huge influence of this political defeat on his writing but also his transformation from a classical poet into a Nimaic, or Modernist poet (after Nima Youshij), giving his work absolute prominence in Persian Poetry.

His poetics also contains an internal struggle taking place within language itself between idiolects, accents, lingua franca, archaic language, vernacular slang and neologisms. For instance, in (the poem I translated), the word *Shirinaabhaa*,[4] in the original, is a combination of "Shirin" (sweet) and "aabhaa" (water). I have translated it as **"sweetwaters"**. One should know that this neologism conveys the same effect as it has in Persian: the invented word signifies an unidentifiable but nonetheless palpable phenomenon. In this case, by combining the word "sweet" with "water" he suggests that uncanny moment when you feel the tide is on your side. You are winning easily, so the game is sweet.

The poem, 'Then, After Thunder'[5] (1959) uses a combination of modern, classical and invented meter, constantly making and breaking different patterns. It is not only Akhavan's language that oscillates between the archaic, the contemporary, the visceral and at times the vulgar, but the metrics themselves switch back and forth as well. To be loyal to the spirit of this constant shifting between registers and metrics, I chose to follow a pattern of occasional rhyme that constantly makes and breaks itself. This experimental translation attempts to evoke Akhavan's manoeuvring between registers and invented meters without any attempt to replicate it.

While translating Akhavan, I was mindful that the structure of the text should adapt to the mytho-historical epic form he uses. However, the melancholic and at times humorous tone of his poem was at odds with the epic and apocalyptic English texts from which I borrowed words. Rather than producing word-for-word replicas, I have preserved Akhavan's penchant for archaic words by scattering similarly obsolete English words throughout this translation.

* *

---

[4] شیرین آبها
[5] Mehdī Akhavān Sāless, *Az in avestā, 1339–1344* (Tehrān: Entesharāt-e Morvārid. 1977) p. 40

Persian literature has survived many oppressive regimes over centuries by poets habitually obscuring the true meaning of their works through coding. Readers of Persian poetry immediately look for 'other' levels of meaning in a text.[6] What might read like a lyrical Sufi poem, for example, may carry political and/or spiritual codes. Akhavan's poetics, moving between classical and modern verse, push this equivocality to its fullest.

The continuing impact of the 1953 coup in contemporary Iran, makes this poem timely and relatable to its Iranian readers. In what follows, I will go through the poem stanza by stanza to reveal some of the codes used. In this decoding of Akhavan's poem, my aim is to explore the untranslatability of lived politics, such as to be found in this man's reflections on the 1953 *coup d'état*. Every incident in the poem corresponds to an incident from the day of the coup.

Stanza II – **The wolf.** In his well-known poem 'the song of wolves and dogs' (1951)[7] written after Sándor Petőfi, Omid depicts 'us' as rebellious wolves dying of *our* wounds. These wounds are the price of our freedom. Given the success of that poem and its immediacy in readers' minds, the wolf-narrator can be understood as being the poet himself. In his poems, Omid, Iran and Mosadeq are used interchangeably.

The hyena is used colloquially as a pejorative reference to Western imperial influence in Iran, with the 'old hyena' meaning the United Kingdom. The term has been used by Iranians after each of the three British-led famines in Iran, but most commonly after the famine of 1919. The term has been used in Iranian poetry of resistance after the constitutional revolution.

---

[6] Also, permutations of words in a verse to initiate equivocal reading is common-place in Persian modern and classical writing and is a nightmare for translators. Sometimes the translator must unpack them a bit to ease the flow of the poem. I have left them as they are for the reader to decide how they want to interpret them. For instance, "my dreams, tamed waters of terror" is just as ambiguous here as it is in the original.

[7] Mehdi Akhavān Sāless, *Zemestān: majmū-e she'r* (Tehrān: Enteshārāt-e Morvārīd. 1996), 53.

Stanza III – In the Iranian imagination, the nationalisation of Iranian oil and the process of cutting off oil royalty advances is repeatedly figured as cutting off the hands of imperialism.[8] The **two hands cut off from the elbow** might therefore refer to the two influential arms of the UK and the US, since the *coup d'état* was a collaboration between MI6 and the CIA, with the CIA playing an orchestrating role. This assumption comes from the hands shutting the door and sealing them with the bloody sign of a claw (visually crown-like, referencing both the British crown and the claws of the hyena).

Stanza IV – Many critics, Manouchehr Atashi[9] and Abdolali Dastgheib[10] among them, interpret the **albino** as the evil spirit of history with Dastgheib also hinting that it might also be the evil spirit of imperialism.

The **light in the neighbour's house** was used prevalently by Iranian leftist poets of the time to symbolise the influence of the Soviet Union in Iran.

Stanza V – The absence of the **King** on the chessboard indicates the flight of the Shah on the day of the coup.

Stanza VI – The cold alien tone of the **parrot** which repeats what is dictated to it and may refer to the BBC's role in airing the code word that sparked the coup.

Stanza VII – All the statesmen involved in the implementation of the coup took refuge in the US and UK embassies after the thunder/coup, seeking shelter **from the Iblīs** (a Quranic reference to Satan).

---

[8] Mohammad Ali Movahed, *Khāb-e Ashofte-y Naft: Doctor Mosadeq va Nehzat-e Melli-e Iran*, Vol.1 (Tehran: Nashr-e Kārnāmeh, 1999), 840.

[9] Manūchehr Ātashí, *Akhavān Shāʿerí ké Sheʿrash Būd* (Tehran: Nashr-e Amytis, 2003), 95.

[10] Abulalí Dastgheib, *Negāhí bé Mehdi Akhavān Sāless* (Tehran: Enteshārāt-e Morvārīd, 1994), 251.

Akhavān Sāless, Mehdi. *Ākhar-i Shāhnāmah: majmū-e she'r.* Tehran: Morvārīd, 1996.

Akavān Sāless, *Mehdi Az īn avestā: Mağmūeh-ye še'r 1339–1344.* Tehran: Morvārīd, 1977.

Akhavān Sāless, Mehdi. *Tuŕā ay kuhan būm ū bar dūst dāram: majmūah-'i shi'r.* Tehran: Morvārīd, 1992.

Akhavān Sāless, Mehdi. *Zemestān: majmū'ah-'i shi'r.* Tehrān: Morvārīd, 1996.

Ātashī, Manouchehr. *Akhavan Shāerī ke Sherash Bud.* Tehran: Nashr-e Amytis, 2003.

Dastgheyb, Abdulalī. *Negāhi be Mehdi Akhavān Sāleth.* Tehran: Morvārīd, 1994.

Movahed, Mohammad Ali. *Khāb-e Ashofte-y Naft: Doctor Mosadeq va Nehzat-e Melli-e Iran*, Vol. 1. Tehran: Nashr-e Kārnāmeh, 1999.

Mehdi Akhavan Saless (M. Omid)

Translated from Persian by Ghazal Mosadeq

آنگاه پس از تندر

اما نمی دانی چه شبهایی سحر کردم
بی آنکه یک دم مهربان باشند با هم پلکهای من
در خلوت خواب گوارایی.
و آن گاهگه شبها که خوابم برد،
هرگز نشد کاید به سویم هاله ای، یا نیمتاجی گل
از روشنا گلگشت رویایی.

Transliteration:

amā nemīdānī ché shabhāyy sahar kardam.

bī ānké yekdam mehrbān bāshand bā ham pelk-hā-ye man

dar khalavat-e khāb-e govārāyy

va ān gāhgah shabhā ké khābam bord

hargez nashod kāyad bé sūyam hālé-ey yā nim-tājī gol

az roshanā golgasht-e ro'yāyy

Then, After Thunder

Yet little
You know of those nights kept vigil
No calm of a dream serene
My two eyelids never so kind as to share
A wee touch

Those sparse nights though
           That I slept
No wreath, no flower halo
From illuminated wandering dreams
Ever came
                To me

My dreams
Tamed waters of terror
Flash convoys of dread and delirium
As far as the eye
             Can see

*

Who is this? A wolf in extremis
A wound on its neck
Its life playing out
Keens its own myths through
A soundbox of a dying body,
                   dolefully

And this? A hyena out of a pit
Satiated and stiff on a corpse
               exhumed.

Its gaze indifferent
To me
        Rubs its snout in filth

Then, two dead hands, cut-off-at-the-elbow
Come to the fore   in a hail of slaps
I hie to the doors I see
Open, but someone's bloody claw
Unclear whose
Shuts the door watertight
      The moment I reach it

An owlish albino fiend turns up
         Cackles
Points to those closed doors sealed with the sign
Of a sanguine claw

Her index finger sways
        To scare

She says:
"Sit.
Chess."

An array of bishops, rooks and knights
Pounce on me as if in a flood
I feel as if
     I jerk awake

A leaf in a gale my heart shakes
Or like a waterdoused blaze
Howlful in its hushed drowning
Its death

I soothe myself then, that was a reverie, a figment
And yet

If I'm chilling waiting
                    a sweet sneer
                Of morn morrow
No bosom, no lullaby will ever soothe
A soul jumping like a yelping child with night terrors

***

One of many times

Night and blackout
Or daylight, or when, I can't recall
But suppose I saw loads of light
Inside the neighbours' hall

Maybe lamplit, maybe daylight
Maybe neither,   anyway
On our rooftop, on a bleary dark kilim,
With a yellow haired spinster who mirrored
My wife,   in too many ways,
In a chessbattle
        I submerged

One dearly warm sweet war
My mind awake
        A vigilant conqueror

What is more, the luck was pouring into my lap
For
I had felled several of her arrogant
Galloping cavalry
        In my expanding attacks

The game was in its sweetwaters
Yet my heart in an unsung fear
Shook in a constant quiver

It was about to betray me it seemed
An eye of mine or a limb
But my rival trembled
Even more than me

In the last gasps of the game,
My wife,
My playmate in gruesome chess,
     That endless yayless chess,
Burst into a sudden cackle
Spilling shivers down my spine
     Say she also made me laugh a little

     I saw no King on her board

She said:

"Come checkmate these castles"

     She laughed

"Meaning?"

     Said I.

Laughingly she made this response:

"You shan't checkmate me, I know."

Old wise greybeards slyly laugh together
I see floods of blood and tears
In their titters.

A sickly yellow parrot out yonder
Repeated all she said
In a cold alien cadence:

"You shan't checkmate me, I know"

Then she pulled a dead knight
                              Out of the carnage
Pointed to the sky with it   between south and east
Thence she gestured to
The spectral advance
                Patch of cloud,

Saying:

"There"

I asked:

"There what?"

She rubbed her palms together

I asked one more time.

She whined hard in hate

"You shall see."

Suddenly I made it out.

Rumbling thunder crashed
Between south and east
Lightning cracked a flash
Then rain lashed

Everything and everywhere wet
Everyone fugitive towards a roof,
          be it the roof of a ne'er-do-well
Or towards an umbrella,
          be it the umbrella of the Iblīs

With my own wife I stood thunderbolt
On our rooftop,   on a dark kilim
Under the rain
          Say, I also shed a tear

In the gory realm
                    of that dreamchess
That spirited serious game
These sugared pieces,
                    sweets,
                              dulcet deeds
And this avalanching cloud?

There, there was a flame,
                    It died
Here a depressed gleam

Under a cascade of blood
                    A hurling downpour
Who will be that fearless again
To risk
          on another rooftop,
          on another kilim,
Yet another game?

Those expansions, those formations
Those elephants, knights, and towers

The pelt of rain and the plaint of gutters

All collapsing roofs

I regret the too high roof
                of our naïve dreams
That fecund grove
                Its trees
From all corners morphed
Into our crosses

***

As if the cloud wept inside me
Damp and drowsy, I

        In my throat, an umbrella unfurling its claws

As if the cloud wept inside me

Erín Moure

Translating Chus Pato

Chus Pato's Galician is an activation in thinking and in muscular force. To take her poetry from Galician, with its rich history of radical lyricism (the medieval *cantigas* of Iberia), of protest (Ferrín), of feminism and philosophy (de Castro), and of modernity (Antonio) into English is at times to founder. I have to build bridges while listening carefully. I "intranslate" Pato: absorb her and attempt to retain her particularity and accent as I speak her words in the language that I learned as a child in western Canada, English. The "globality" of English always already risks removing the writer's particular accent. It is a challenge.

Inhabiting her poetry is to inhabit a language given explosive density, pressing on the verb instead of the subject pronoun, a language in which self-reflexivity is *not* self-absorbed. Connections between place and land, natality and birthplace, and the possibility of voice and language are tangible in the forms and content, in the pulsations, sounds, movements of Pato's poems. Here are history, ancient rivers, Psyche, gesture, theatre, characters, stones, birds, trees, waters, women not haunted but haunting, namings, danger, freedom.

I work to resolve the usual problems translators resolve, in which cultural iconography is unrecognizable and needs added vocables. A "124"? It's an affordable 1960s sedan built by the state firm SEAT in Francoist Spain under license from Fiat, and for villagers caught in that dictatorship, it represented freedom of movement. In English, I can never achieve the poetic reverberation of suppositions, views, politics, repressions, land, and of release from claustrophobia that I receive in reading those three numerals in Pato's poem. As I have said (in *Insecession*) to Chus Pato: *I can only intranslate you*, translate across a self, produce a version that relies on the gulf or gap just as it abhors it.[11] I try to interfere minimally, so I add "SEAT" to the English, and perhaps 124 will now mean a car! Though the initials of *Sociedad Española de Automóviles de Turismo* also resonate, alas, as merely a place

---

[11] Erín Moure, *Secession/Insecession* (Toronto: BookThug Press, 2016), 8.

to sit down. In a similar vein of problematic, there is the alphabetic order of her poem 'Stalker,' echoing Andrei Tarkovsky's momentous film, of course, yes, but here it is the alphabet itself (and thus writing) that is a trail not subject to the laws of physics, and the poet the stalker who leads us into the Zone, then vanishes. Here I had to keep the alphabet marching along: "gorxa" became "gorget" instead of "throat," and the scientific *nymphaeaceae* appears at first for water lily because it starts with "n." What is found in the forest of the poem is "one's most cherished desire," echoing not Pato's formulation exactly, but the English subtitles that translate those words on the screen from Russian in the Tarkovsky film. So as to draw the connection closer.

Yes, these are issues all translators meet and resolve. The challenges in Pato lie not just in the relation between languages and cultures, but also that in the culture of origin there is already a fraught relationship between Galician the language, Galicians the people, and the Spanish state in which Galicia lies. Centralist politics and landholding policies have for centuries abused the Atlantic lands of Galician presence to extract resources and people from Galicia and suppress their language and culture, a process that accelerated in the nineteenth century and is still ongoing. The land has many ghosts – like the vast prairie lake of the Antela in Pato's ancestral Limia, drained in the 1950s for farmland (today, Limian potatoes, the *Pataca de Galicia*, have an EU protected geographic indication (PGI)). The draining of the lake, as well as marking a loss of tradition, flora, and language, marks the surge of a capitalist ethos in which profit and export take precedence over language and community.

These heightened issues of positionality accompany my every translational move, especially in English, language of absorptive capital. I work to transfer into English not just sounds and meanings but the kinetics of Pato's poetic relation between family, friends, love, emotion, capital, language, and the air and fire and earth and water, the birds and beings – all things that give her poetry a sensation of the prophetic, of the inter- and post-postapocalyptic that – as it turns out – human beings are living everywhere.

The intranslatable, in Pato, is the "unreaderly" that burns in the mouth.[12] I have to transfer these to a North American mouth, an English

---

[12] Erín Moure, *Insecession*, 8

mouth… a mouth with muscles and fibres not the same, a history of cells not the same. What to do with those taut torques in Galician that deeply affect how language infests its speaker, how language itself *creates* a speaker? That Galician propositions or phrases do not need personal pronouns before verbs (unless to emphasize or avoid unproductive ambiguity) means a subject is indicated inside a verb declension, and thus is often not gendered as it pulses "in the act." In English the person is gendered right from the start, as if gender's scaffold were crucial to any communication about the world. In Galician, there's room to just be a person. Further, there are the echoes and registers of the illocutionary acts held and transmitted in words: in English and in Galician the forces are different. Thinking is different. To make things happen in words is not EXACTLY the same as in English. An intranslatable, then, is not a word, or a phrase, or an expression, but a movement between mouth/muscle/person-speaker and their relation with a push/act/articulation/thinking. It is this movement that torques each word, each syllable or sound at the centre or core of an utterance, that must be translated, or intranslated, along with the word. It's not simply a culture and history that differ. Something deeper changes as the poem moves into the new language. How to catch this? You have to first let it alter the old you, in a way. As a translator, I come unstuck from my self in this change of codes, mysteries, time. A timing. Time itself is altered in the poem. It's the only way I really have of describing it. To struggle with the inconnection of time's lattice is one way that the intranslatable, and the need to intranslate – like a fire that burns in the mouth – comes into play when I work to bring Pato's time and words into English.

Chus Pato, too, intranslates even as she is writing, because she can't be explained according to the old keys. Pato's work has been called "hermetic," though she is not hermetic, she is an absolute materialist, it's revolutionary what she does. Translating her changes my relation to English, to the Englishes, to my place and time and thus affects my own poetry. And affects the poetry of others, too, when they read Chus Pato on either side of the Atlantic in English translation. Our poetics change, possibility changes for us too, when we get a homeopathic dose of Pato, either via translation, or via the readings and works of those who have read her.

To quote Galician critic Arturo Casas writing on Chus Pato's *m-Talá*, though his words can be extrapolated to all her poetry (and I translate): "It's a civil poetry made in a new language, devastating, tenacious, vigorous, scarcely cantabile or communicative but powerfully elaborated and lucid, resistant to the bootprint of historical circumstance."[13]

It helps us construct a future. Wherever we are. *A gorget, a gorgeousness*. Zone. It's up to you.

---

[13] Arturo Casas, "Chus Pato: m-Talá," *A Trabe de Ouro*, no. 44, tomo IV, ano XI, outuro-novembro-decembro (Santiago de Compostela: Sotelo Blanco Edicións, 2000), 545-551. Reprinted in Chus Pato. *Obra completa*. Volume extra. *m-Talá*. Edición do vixésimo aniversario (Vigo: Euseino? Editores, 2020), 139-146.

Chus Pato

Translated from Galician by Erín Moure

There are images that wall off the body
from the violence of the body
they're outside memory
spread out like the strata of an exemplary life
fed by roe deer
in the forests of Brabant
the bloodbath happens
To stand up reeling in the mist
and head somewhere else
interminable
the law meeting up and passing the signs of time

In the same way
that birds, carved in basalt, emit from their eyes
a pulsar of emerald
so fragments of rock-language
pulverized, fly up over an ocean

against you

we are the pulsar of birds
linguistic rock
all potency any virtuality
an infinite exposure
an infinity of pain

there's nowhere we cross paths with you

The photographs are very similar
in both a woman is posed with her daughters
who are very young
One woman is my grandmother
the other a woman assassinated in '36
the young girls each lived on different continents
and never felt the joy of a reunion
At night a voice comes
"they snatched her from me"
it's the voice of an old woman
the doors of death are open to her
A boy
in his haste
falls down and scrapes himself day after day
until his body vanishes
The old woman and the boy walk
hand in hand in a dawn
they're lost in the hinterlands of time

Self-Portrait
or Encounter with Gesture and Ancient Psyche

If you watch me in the mirror
you'll see poplars
toward sunrise a park
at its top, urban structures,
toward sunset the waters run freely
and the trees bunch in oakwoods
or are dome for the river
the fields soak up water and reflect wintry skies
behind them, industrial zones.
If you catch me in profile in the mirror
you'll see that I wake facing south
and the blankets pull irresistibly north.
Dürer painted the pillow he slept on six times
as if to decipher the rhythm of images that only come with eyes shut tight
If you face the mirror
you'll see a bus disgorging tourists who look around with interest
you'll see an old woman very upright
she prays and accompanies her prayer with movements that are in
        themselves a rite
she's not praying because she thinks that my breath is about to leave
        my body
she prays because she knows that the words of prayer alleviate pain
she moves because she knows that gesture and dance are more
        ancient than words.
No, what I saw wasn't death
who I saw was Time
I saw its feet and its legs, it wore peter-pan stockings and took off
naturally
I saw the hem of its cape, a short cape
that's what I saw.
If the spirit were to have a centre
that's where it'd gather the burst of fifty thousand throat-slit buffalo

it has no centre
it expands through each and every pore of the psyche which is blind
and is archaic and precedes gesture
and precedes the sequence of stockinged legs and short cape,
no?
My dreams face the south
because I sleep on my right side so as not to press on the heart
sacred and ardent heart
Aië, heart!!!

Ethos

It's true that from green to black we can't draw a chromatic diameter
    with grey at its centre
but those were the colours

the slippers gleamed on the parquet
sign of your solitude

we tend to link the anachronistic with the past
but what survives does not allow closure
the celestial that enveloped you

at dawn we followed the course of creeks
and the lunar green that grows on oaks
All was grey
the emerging plants
the feet that hold up your weight
the abundance

                    *

As for colours, I'm ready for them all
        we can't follow the course of the breath from lunar green to the
        celestial
but yes, we can plant a mandarin tree
and use its orange to breathe out to the sky

        in the lichen, as it's autumn, the burnished red of the oaks is white
        violet is the liver and yellow the sunlight

                the centre could be grey
                like some dolmen
                and a river
                where all is forgotten

                        *

I didn't enter the room
I saw the slippers from the doorway
if I murmur in your ear
"I come from the night"
I say "the night's not going to leave"

                        *

An arrow is a line between two points that directs somewhere

        we produce a vertex
        a vertex of ice

when released, the arrow points to the earth
Earth's indications are symbolized by a pendulum
and by scales
if we can manage to save gravity the vertices will align
        ice azimuth // volcano or fire azimuth

outside the law opposites cease to reveal the contradictory ambition
           of consciousness as lava or volcano
           of the mind as integral to earthly morphogenesis
           as in the sequence: lava, vapor, water, ice

we trace out a circuit of levitation
burbling water
water running freely to the oceans
mercury

there we pin the compass needle

where we're located there's no contradiction, the diameters are three
and point nowhere

           from bile yellow or sunlight to violet
           from lunar lichen to the red or bronze of autumns
           from mandarin orange to the celestial that enveloped you

           the *ethos* or centre-point is grey

in it all the radii of this wheel converge without start or end

where we're located: fraying a path through the fog
inside a cloud
in mirrors

           ethos can be read as chromatic temperament
           it's the possibility of an appearance
           the possibility that colours will make an appearance

lightly without gravity
which indicates that the scales are inoperative
that bodies located there are free from judgement

the variations are slight but unceasing and forceful

*

The celestial that envelops you can't be/does not allow
closure
it's time that travels in time and survives a period of danger

*

Memory bursts open, it's important because it activates the starting point
two people who love each other and decide to live together
the rest of their lives
they live aside huge blockfields of granite
or in the foothills of the central cordillera
in green lands / so green they're blue
Atlantic norwesters are unleashed from there
and black diamonds glint
they agree on a language whose words bear the time that
travels in Time: its anachronisms
and suspends what's now happening
they, the lovers, are archaic
as love is

marigolds or impatiens can be planted instead of the mandarin tree

*

Memory's born with the weight of desire, it corresponds to the period
in which the protagonists were dismantled by an image and saw their
lives destroyed, each to each

*

Concentration runs up against time

       like wedding bands for the flight
       for the long voyage of images in times of danger

       may time fly like crows
       on the bluest of wings

or how they're on the move, as if space were a manuscript
signed Jan Potocki
in the olive-green SEAT 124, *Caballo prieto azabache* cranked
up full blast
analogously I entered your heart
you read the stories of Lovecraft

       like bands or rings or levitational spheres

       or the dead (women/men) above the waters

stalker

::::: anthracite
::::: belladonna   *purpurea*
::::: carbuncle
::::: digitalis
::::: let them draw near
::::: foxglove
::::: gorget
::::: Timurid pentalogy   *Herat*
::::: ithyphallic – standing stone – Limia/Lascaux
::::: k
::::: L ::::: M
::::: semicircular curve that shields wanderers caught by unexpected
    showers
    nymphaeaceae

> *Water lily is the usual name of the Nymphaeaceae*
> *that in Galician is* nenúfar *or* ninfea, *and in French,*
> nénuphar *or* nymphéa. *Any tourist who's curious can see*
> *Monet's* Nymphéas *in the Orangerie, by the Jeu de Paume.*
> *The Jeu de Paume has a pediment that claims in part that*
> *Basque lands of Nafarroa Beherea, Lapurdi and Zuberoa*
> *belong to the French State. Any Limian, tourist or emigrant*
> *in Paris say in the 40s of the last century, would translate*
> *the title of Monet's paintings as* As auganas. **Augana** *is the*
> *word Limians used and maybe still do, for a water lily, back*
> *when they bloomed in the Antela. Born when the Antela*
> *was drained, we never saw such flowers; yet often we heard a*
> *voice alive or dead utter* augana *and in the eyes of memory*
> *we'd glimpse the referent afloat on the waters.*

::::: letter that shepherds use to fend off April showers and thunder-
    storms of May
::::: second surname of my father
::::: first surname of my father
::::: emirates – is she still alive?

:::: constellation of the Stalker

> *The houses are two, deep in a forest, and in them one's most cherished desires are fulfilled. In one house the hero throttles a possessed woman, on his return he crosses paths with the constellation of the Antichrist and realizes that **reynard**, crow, and doe can be redeemed too. The Stalker slips out of the forest edge or "primordial nature"; the bodies of women burned through the ages head to the peaks. Hallowed ones.*

:::: Stalker
:::: Tarkovsky
:::: u
:::: v for victory / plovgh
:::: w for arrowhead / plow
:::: unknown
:::: path that bifurcates
:::: Zone

Zoë Skoulding

Half Bird: Translating Music and Noise

I first crossed paths with Frédéric Forte at a Double Change reading in Paris, at which he read, at great speed, a poem that took me by surprise when his quickfire French was interrupted by a word in Welsh, the name of my neighbouring village Llanfairpwllgwyngyllgogerychwyrndrobwllllantysiliogogogoch. The poem in question comes from the same collection as the poems I have translated here, *Dire ouf* (Paris: P.O.L., 2016), which reveal Forte as a poet who is relentlessly curious about sound. *Dire ouf* is a homophonic translation of Deerhoof, the San Francisco indie band – one that playfully exaggerates the sound of the name with a French accent. It reveals an ongoing investigation into noise, the point where sound and signification are pushed towards what exceeds music and song. It also recalls the French expression *ne pas avoir le temps de dire ouf*, which is similar to phrases in English like not having time to catch your breath, or something happening before you know what has hit you – and this is often the effect of Forte's writing.

The question of how to think about poetry in relation to music is one that has always fascinated me. Having also played music, like Forte, who was a musician before he was a poet, I sometimes miss the interaction with others when I'm writing poetry, the interaction of playing in a group – even if the writing of poetry already involves tuning in to other voices and texts. This is what drew me to translation in the first place: my first experiences of translating poetry were in collaborative workshops organised by Literature Across Frontiers, where the process of arriving at a translation often seemed secondary to the conversation around it.[1] I have not worked in that way with Forte, although he has provided some helpful notes along the way, but the pleasure of translation is immersion in a different sound and communal encounter through the text, the sense of being between languages. My first translations of his work were made for his readings

---

[1] Ingmara Balode, Julia Fiedorczuk, Sanna Karlström, Ana Pepelnik, Zoë Skoulding, Sigurbjörg Thrastardottir and Elżbieta Wójcik-Leese, *Metropoetica* (Bridgend: Seren, 2013).

in Wales, with an ear to reading alongside him, finding the sound that would match his French performance in English. His poems, in turn, enter music with a collaborative listening, not to represent music mimetically but to respond to it within a parallel structure.

As a member of Oulipo, the *Ouvroir de littérature potentielle*, Forte has a wide range of techniques at his disposal, developed over this group's existence since 1960, and he has added many constraints of his own. The one he uses here is derived from the poet and mathematician Jacques Roubaud, one of Oulipo's most longstanding and influential members. Based on the syllabic counts of the haiku and tanka and an extension of their principle to numbers beyond five and seven, each line must have a number of syllables (as well as each stanza a number of lines and a total number of syllables) that adds to a prime number, and in this poem the structure is decided regarding the duration of the related Deerhoof songs. As the poem is completely structured by this constraint, I have used it in the translation, yet it produces something quite different from the replication of a traditional verse form. The expression is interrupted and swerved by the irregular syllable counts; rather than creating a form that seems natural or inevitable, the constraint draws attention to the arbitrary shape of language in relation to the flux of experience. The acknowledgements in *Dire ouf* inform the reader that the poems were composed while listening to Deerhoof albums, including the four that give their names to the poems here. These are poems that engage with an open-ended listening, one that is receptive to the chaotic range of sense impressions and multiplying significations; it is a listening across languages, not just to lyrics but to a particular post-punk or noise pop musical sensibility. The *Reveille* of the album title in French becomes "Wake Up" in Forte's poem, and then turns back to French in my translation. Forte's poem is not a translation of lyrics, but of sound – the noisiness of everything that exceeds lyric expression.

What draws me to this work is the way that it hovers on the edge of chaos while pursuing a rigorous mathematical pattern. It resists absorption into meaning, while engaging in a conversational relation with the reader that makes a space for daydream, memory and childlike playfulness. Its energy comes from the friction between music and poetry. "It's an insult to poetry to call it song. It's an insult to song to call it poetry," writes Roubaud in opposition to poetry that, in his view, fails to engage with the essential doubleness of poetry as both written and oral form, doubled again by the reader's experience of a work that is both textually and aurally received.[2] Deerhoof's songs, in which the lyrics sung by Satomi Matsuzaki are fully integrated into the sonic textures and rhythmical complexity of music, gain nothing from being described as poetry, despite their verbal originality. Forte's poems are not performance pieces, in the sense of being written specifically for oral performance, but they enact a performance of listening on the page, one in which the zig-zagging irregularities of the music are reflected in his stop-start lines. Images overflow syntactical units; white space is both interruption and silence: white noise. The publication of Forte's book in 2016 led to collaboration with two members of Deerhoof, Greg Saunier and John Dieterich, who wrote a piece to accompany Forte's reading of new work the following year. However, the distance between poetry and music, in activating different modes of listening, is as important as their synergies.

The space between song and poetry is, as Roubaud indicates, risky ground. There may be a certain mistrust of the encounter between French poetry, with its distinctive relationship to particular traditions, and the commercial juggernaut of American rock. At the same time, French poetry has derived its contemporary energy from an intense exchange with the poetry of the USA since the 1960s, as Abigail Lang has explained in her book *La conversation transatlantique: Les échanges franco-américains en poésie depuis 1968* (Dijon: Les presses du réel, 2021). She identifies two influences, one of them literality, particularly in the use of citational approaches, but also a renewed interest in orality that derives in turn from US poetry's counter-cultural connections with music and performance throughout the late twentieth century. Both of these are evident in *Dire ouf*, and in the tensions it enacts on the page.

Deerhoof's music, like much of the music I enjoy most, is balanced between music and noise, or precision and chaos, to the extent that these binaries are unsustainable. Similarly, the mathematical rigour of a constraint subverts and estranges the expected musicality of the poem. There is a sense of exerting control over sound, but also, like a dancer, being controlled by it. The poet is, like the musician, half

---

[2] Craig Dworkin and Marjorie Perloff, eds., *The Sound of Poetry / The Poetry of Sound* (Chicago: University of Chicago Press, 2009), 18.

bird: half responding to a sensory environment, and half responding to the cultural frame of song. The superb lyre bird who makes an appearance at the end of Forte's poem makes no distinction between mimicry of its own kind and of human machinery. The gap between birdsong and pneumatic drill, where both exist in a continuity of sonic experience, makes the poem audible as an articulation of the material world that is also part of it. In translating to the poem's constraint, I find something like the experience of playing music, which is not the self-expression it is often thought to be, but exactly the opposite, a pleasure in resonating structures that put language into the same continuum as the world it describes.

Frédéric Forte

Translated from French by Zoë Skoulding

from *Dire ouf*

Moitié oiseau

conversation vient
de très loin
, au-dehors c'est la
guerre / toi
tu es si

léger, légère : oh!
(flûte à bec)
– et quelqu'un s'énerve
puis se calme
se re-calme

, rêve dans les plumes
d'un mobile au plafond comme
d'un ange au plafond
/ y a un ressort, une boîte
qui nous font nous
endormir

– même nuit, un nid
un lit double sur mesure
et on imagine
dans la chambre, qui déferle
une école de poissons –

comment appelait-
on ces sons
-là au Moyen Âge ?

(au milieu
              de la vie)

                              glockenspiel ?
       même pas, peut-être
                      « des flocons »

              – ou monter
                          une expédition
       dans les branches
                      et s'apercevoir
                              qu'on vit là depuis

                          depuis toujours, face
              au soleil
                          même quand il frappe
(dans le temps)
                      à rebours –

              alors, si oiseau
                          en mode nocturne, je
       suis parmi les choses
                          retenues et la menace
       sourde peut porter dans une

              autre langue un autre
                          nom : qui n'est pas *tsunami*
       – « cette ritournelle
                  sait résister à des vents
       dépassant, etc. »

              , posée sur un fil
       chante en boucle
                          chante en boucle chante
              jusqu'à être
                      dénudée

– on part d'une ligne
              et produit du sentiment
         électrique avec

             trois fois rien /
un petit sauvage
           dans sa salle

                de bains – l'aventure
        pourrait se terminer là
             mais ceci encore
(coda en forme de post-
        script) : dans les forêts
            du Sud-Est australien le
        ménure superbe *
imite à la perfection
        les sons : chants des autres
oiseaux naturels et même
le bruit du marteau-piqueur

* oiseau-lyre

Halfbird

conversation in
the distance
, outside it may be
war / but you
you are so

light boy/girl light: oh!
(recorder)
and someone's wound up
then calms down
calm again

, dreams in feathers of
a mobile on the ceiling
like an angel on
the ceiling / there's a spring, a
box that sends us off to sleep

– the same night, a nest
made-to-measure double bed
and you imagine
a school of fish rising from
its benches, flooding the room

what would you call these
sounds there in
the Middle Ages
(in the mid-
dle of life)

glockenspiel?
not really, maybe
"falling snow"

              – or mounting
                   an expedition
     in branches
          and then realising
              that you'd always lived

        there always, facing
    into the
        sun even when it
hits (in time)
        runs backwards –

    so, if I'm bird in
        the nocturnal mode, then I'm
among remembered
        things and the hidden danger
can in another language

    carry another
            name: which is not tsunami
– "this little refrain
      is able to resist winds
exceeding, etc."

     , balanced on a thread
   sing in loops
        sing in loops singing
     until you're
       stripped naked

    you start with a line
          and produce an electric
      emotion with three

        times nothing /
   a little savage
      in the bath-

room – the adventure
could terminate right there but
there is also this
(coda in the form of post-
script): in the forests
of South-East Australia
the superb lyrebird
perfectly imitates sounds:
natural songs of
other birds and even the
sound of the pneumatic drill

Reveille

telephone: listen
if it (rings)
it rings and why not

isolate ambient noise
because of (your ears)
/zero replacement unit
this could be such a
terrible drama

minuscule
"no, none of the i's
is dotted"

– here undertake the precise description of
the bones of the inner ear
which resemble some of the letters you have

(bird's eye view)
noted? an Inuit
impression,

an ululation –
"there I want everything to
repeat itself, to

repeat precisely" which is to say never
to be exactly the same
writing us in waves like a History of
Melodic Invention Through
the Ages (insert image here) – make sure it
keeps going and doesn't stop
anything but that: do not

stop / the pop organ, voice: it's
always beautiful
to be eight years old, no? fixed

stare fixes
        time to the mirror
, suspended

        – or you're hairy for
            the very first time reading
old comics, a (form

        of experience)
                Johann Sebastian Bach's
        method of living

        / a great deal of noise in the garage the walls
are sound are fully soundproofed:
                and electricity has been discovered

            – scratch! tranquillity
                        runs as a river in the
            forest the very
                    matter of sleep, ripped pillows
        fall apart or make
(make like this) apparently
        / these little mechanical

        dolls on strings
    : monkeys on the drums
            menacing

        seized up but only joking –
whistling on the way
        no big deal see it's nothing
etc. the
        nursery rhyme count

            – coming to end in (beauty)
                in levitation / centimetres above
            the ground and then slowing down
                    the why of it so clear and how clearly you
        say it: a morning waking, we're waking up

Offend Maggie

can we get everything out through the window?
                              the question of the great spring
            tidy-up: whole house that takes to the air in
a fully-sealed tornado
                              / and the drum of the washing machine before
            it comes to rest and before
                        we can rest – it's a bedside

            scene from a novel
                              of adventures in the head
            "now we are dragons,
                        we're knights-in-armour-ish things"
            the forest in us
                  that we cross without moving
: there are secrets – a wrinkle

                        , an iridescence
in the surface: a little
                  piece of you glimpsed be-
                              tween three overlapping states
            (the substance changes)
                  how to put it? something that
I will never become – to

                        be the cavalry
      always and
            always turn up far
                              too late (but
                  with a smile)

            / archaic version
                  of me: great
            windmills of my arms
                        a bit like
                  Pete-Townshend-

who-wouldn't-destroy-
                anything – in the low times
        I learn to take aim
                : throw elastic bands towards
        the wastepaper basket – it's

                all easy: warm days
        cyclical
                (what are you thinking?)

                – seen from a certain angle truly the world
is a form of perfection
                , a book of my son's in which a bear squeezes
        all the trees between its paws
                all the animals (*Big Bear Hug* its name is)
        how after that to avoid
                becoming sentimental?

                        – anyway don't take
        my word for it, inexact
                at every turn
        / then shifting up a gear or
                two (fireworks in the bedroom)

                our voices: 1, 2,
        3 – urgent or not really
                mid-tempo, we are
        indoor spectators of a
                fixed action movie
"until the point when something
        is hammered home" – the rain that

        falls in a sinusoid, object of myself
        swept away by the waves (this
                image again) in the sea of Japan where
the wind of the beginning
        can be found / you take on the form of a kite

you're aerophotographic
          in style as a *rokkaku*

          – a number of signs
inside, words
               translated to hertz

          : there to conceal trans-
               parency, a sharply breath-
                    able air, which is
                         what I am running out of
               / say "a cosmonaut
                    is very precise in a
          vacuum" and lose all fear – *we*

                    has become a little frayed
          pulled in more than one direction its structure
     : DNA, double helix:
                         it's woven, thread by thread, in a tapestry
     quite resistant to frequent
                    wash cycles at 95° (cotton)
and here still on the stove the milk that's boiling over

Breakup Song

and bam! a left hook
in the word
    punching ball / I learn
                  a new kind
            of dance step –

given a machine
            for infra-thin breathing and
    slight continuous
                shifting variations, there
    exists an ideal
            mode of how would you put it?
              friction / it's very simple

                , we both visit the
                    night running on fast forward
        (do you see the lights?)
                a kind of alternative
             nonstop tropicália

                – there's a cable stretched all the way across the
Atlantic, something like a
            memory of the 1980s "what I
        like about the dark myself
            is the stereo effect"

            and all that empties
                  away from our heads the next
            moment – we watch the
        possible worlds passing by
            grasping nothing of
the conversation / we are
            leaning on the bar, fauna

        and flora in confusion
: there comes a point in

the episode where *mirror*
                  ball is equal to
     amnesia (yay)

          "– is this body mine?"
she is wondering, the thought
                  monstrous / from here the

                    theoretical desert
          island solution
                    : shoo! get lost etc.
                       a Robinson who
presents himself with flowers
                       (all this + absence
of telephone) – or

                       put something sexy back in
          your engine, your own
                    private juke-box that flashes
     in the bath "there are
                    days when I feel a little
     like an extremist
                    , and how about you?"

                    / very lost owl in
     Athens: pyjama parties
                    , sirtaki: many
opportunities to chase
          away sad things – a piece of

     good mechanics here: this is
what the heart is for
          in the world in general
     as well as in this
                    particular place / actions
     crowd in and push us
                    to keep moving on

Stephen Watts

Translation as Reversed Gannet

With written or oral texts, it seems to me there is sometimes a sort of ur-language which the text has plunged upwards out of to reach its form at the surface of words. Imagine a reversed gannet at the moment when it has fastened on its food fish, as if it would unwind itself backwards and upwards, the crash of water fusing back into unbroken surface, the bird returned to the sky. Sometimes this is what happens in translation when the writer senses the possible presence of her ur-language in the words or texts of someone else (another writer). And this – I think – is what happened between myself and Ziba Karbassi when, sometime well over twenty years ago, she heard me reading, performing my poetry aloud, and she felt an instinct of possibly shared understanding between her Persian and my English. However unlikely, this is the best way I can express it.

When I co-translate – which I do with many poets & translators – each experience has a different valency and no one way of working will ever be the same or be replicated. Often though – but not always – I think it helps to be in the physical presence of my co-poet/translator(s), so as to sense & to see the poem being bodied forth from them and to catch a first version in its act of becoming. So also the intuition and intensity of questioning is, most often for me, quickened by such presence.

There are things in this process that resist being rationalised but that may be closer to a knot of experienced truth than almost anything else. And friendship is involved: the spirit friendship of shared language. And I stress that it is friendship and I stress the importance of this friendship. It involves, for instance, a "sufism of language", and the energies of that in the explosions of the language are palpable. Here translation is, very precisely, a "love" that is a befriending: a sharing through the empathy of friendship, a sensing that one language stands in equal relation to the other (and perhaps such friendship needs stressing, given how dominant, or hegemonic, English can be).

I think that perhaps dance and some form or sense of music may pre-date language, in which case it is quite likely that poetry also perhaps pre-dates language, and such poetries as pre-date language might be thought of as residing in our experience at a level of ur-language. Of course it is more complicated than that: dance, music, language and poetry surely intermingled over very long periods of time and affected each other back and forth in hybrid and non-sequential ways.

In the Val Camonica that my grandfather was born into (though not the Alta Val Camonica, where he was born, but lower down the valley) there are *rupestri*, or rock carvings, dating back four thousand and more years from where we are now. Some of the carvings seem to depict acts of agriculture and survival, but there are some also that seem more explosive and to do with the occasion of light. The valley where the carvings are found is dominated by a steep limestone mountain that is cleft by a shattering and at certain times the sun, or the moon, or indeed strong stars, can appear to be as if plunging from their unfixities into that cleft. Some *rupestri* seem to be depicting or seeing this, but rather than simply a vision of disappeared light, certain *rupestri* suggest that the people who carved them had understood – perhaps very suddenly – that such light had disappeared into their bodies and could explode again out of their bodies as dance, or that they could *body* light as dance. But when the "gone light" is carved into or onto rock does it become image or language, is it painting or poetry: or rather, is it not both ? Hence also, an explosion of words in the waning light of the world.

The poetry of Ziba Karbassi is rooted in her Tabrizi origins, in the city of Tabriz where she was born with its Azeri, Kurdish and Armenian, as well as Persian inflections. Her poetry (she also writes in Azeri) resides in the rich complexities of her Persian language, for sure, in her closeness to her first teacher (Mohammad Hossein Shahriyar) who she met when she still was a child, and in the swirled explosions and "years of lead" of recent Iranian history, going back let's say to the time of Nima Yushij, or more aptly to the time of Forugh Farrukhzad. In chronological time she was forced to flee Iran with her mother and younger sisters in the early 1980s when she was barely thirteen, following the murder of her stepfather and the stoning to death of a cousin from her wider family. These are among the roots of her poetry, as are the struggle against the unfreedoms of the Islamic Republic and its prison system, the complexities and enervations of the shattered life of exile, where exile always is exile, and the need to take into her body, and thus into the body of her poetry, the destructions of freedom, and the need to placate in language the specifics of unfreedom.

The poems included here were mostly written in the late 2000s, therefore at a time of the irruption of an incipient popular uprising, but one that failed to pre-curse regime change (a change the poet craves in her deep self) and indeed one that was maybe in some ways, sadly, flawed. They coincide also with layers and levels of the harshness of exile (that never leaves) and personal traumas, that the poet – always a poet and knowing that often this was the only thing keeping her alive – sought with great dignity to hold intact in the calmed crisis of her language. Breath is of immense importance to Ziba Karbassi, in terms of her poetry and her poetics as well as her life-breath, as is clear from the brief prose text of hers, "Breath: The Elixir of Poetry", that is included below. Both of us, quite separately, have written short texts on breath and other aspects of poetics – and this text of hers rests close to my own practice as a poet and to my sense of what poetry is or might be. Her poetry also incorporates explosions of light and of language, as mine does too. Such closeness undoubtedly aided, and was a part of, our process of co-translation.

I had some understanding of these things, both from my own sense of what poetry is and from my friendship with the poet. And I want to stress two things: firstly that I (as well as Ziba Karbassi) needed to be a poet, and secondly that we needed to feel some access to a sort of shared ur-language. Without both these "presences" I think we could not have worked on these co-translations in the ways we have, reaching the results we have (or have not) achieved and bringing the Persian poems over into the English we have given them. This is one possible fusion of a work of co-translation. And I would also want to stress this co-translational aspect: if the final English is seen as somehow "mine", it is equally Ziba Karbassi's. These are her poems in English. Ownership, signature, attribution matter less and less and less the more the translations begin to "work". Ego is exploded inside language and poetry's language wins out, if these translations "work" at all.

Ziba Karbassi

Translated from Persian
by Stephen Watts and Ziba Karbassi

Breath: The Elixir of Poetry

Oxygen is the component of air that makes breath possible.

Although it is only one fifth part of air itself, it is that crucial part that makes life possible.

The poet begins the creative process from the body and the senses, from touching and from looking.

It is the concentration on breath that takes the poet to a new level of perception, sharpening sight and hearing. Without this "elixir" of the breath, poetry is like air without oxygen: the living word and energy of poetry is born from the metamorphosis of words that travel along the line of breath.

The "born" poet knows this and so knows how to recreate the word, turning it into a vector of energy : no longer merchandise but "happening", a force capable of lifting off the page and carrying us away.

Language that is rooted in breath knows how to instil the pulse of rhythm into poetry. Or in other words, the pulse of the senses will be infused within language by the poet. This is how poetry becomes a music of the body, how it gradually transforms both the poet and the surrounding world to create a life of its own.

The poetry of breath withholds and accumulates energy within language. And then suddenly it is set off in a leap of the senses. Words fixed in language don't lose their life essence but give birth to one another, as if each word were the open womb of the next. Words that continually and sensually love one another, giving birth to the great emotions : grief, joy, hatred, love, affection, desire, obsession, vulnerability, folly, revenge. For a split second the poet is left breathless : it is in that split second that perception is crystallised around one sensation and, as in a chemical reaction, releases the word.

It is then up to the poet as an expert technician to be able to do the rest.

Diwan Under Snow

Tonight I'm the Kurdest Farzad
from my birth's give & take to my hands' un-razed heist
from the erection of two fingers, the pinkie & fist's first
between all the angles of five & fifty & fifty thousand & fifty million,
to the most Kurdish fourteenth night full moon
of our land's flesh & blood
the heart is shaking
dried lips are shaking
lead of the bullet's chest is shaking
the colour 'no' in your face is shaking
you have neither mother nor sister
nor a home to be bailed back into
not a friend to kick away your gallows stool
not a trigger in your pocket's ripped-out lining,
not even a shroud to be buried in, not a blood home,
no way   you even don't have an even
you don't even have your own shadow
you don't, no you don't, you don't
                    have

two-windowed worry-eyes
warmness of home-fires & chandeliers behind every window
know very well that you're worried about the balcony,

the *diwan* that went sleeping beneath the snows & became crazy
the table that sat down under the snow so as not to appear bare
the woman who white-combed her hair under such snows
poetry poured so pure that the snow lost its white
the loneliness of black-cracked finger-nails
open wounds under ripped-open shirts
the sole witness of the limping roundabouts
that whiplash the horse of an old grocery cart
& end banged up under a bung of limp greens

Death would drown in its own shy sweats
this death if it had feet would flee
if it was human & had a head would bang its head on a tree
or like a stranger-poet from its forearm would fashion a balalaika

and strum it naked under the snows

balalaika   balalaika   bailalaila lala-
    lailai laila-lalai la-lai lie now
        sleep now my lai-lai
            my little one
            my bairn

Sigh Poem 77

Because I was that first woman
Who stood up & danced between drunk
Soldiers & intoxicated chiefs of staff

Sigh Poem 78

Because I was the only one left
Fighting to the last drop of happy blood
So as not to be smelted to iron

Sigh Poem 79

Because you are a man
War will always separate us
Before we are separated by war

Resistance

Wings   shoulder bones   wings   broken bones
Feather   feather   feather   shorn hair
No more   no more colour in her face
No more colour on the face she has at all

No, nothing whatsoever   of this world
From your world   nothing whatsoever at all
She doesn't even know her own name now
She doesn't even know her own name no

Full of bruises   her eyes swollen by blows
Bruises on the thighs   her skin torn
Liver in ashes
With all of this pain
All that's left of her is a scream, a scream
And so – she screams

I am daughter of the first mysteries
Secrets, centuries, origins
I am deaf   dumb   blind
She screams
I'm dumb
And know nothing of nothing

I who stitch threadspans of stars
On the draped robe of night
And put make-up on the face of the moon
I who am laughter yes laughter
Haaa   the laughs I have   haaa
A haa   come from my scream   haaa
And again and again and a third gain
'Til I can take now more and then again
As far as I can go : quick, count the lashings
Ten by ten bone by bone   blackened even
                    unto blackout

Wings shoulder bones   wings   broken bones
Feather feather   feather   shorn hair
No more   no more   colour in her face
No more colour on the face she has at all

Nothing of nothing she has
                    Nothing to tell you
She knows not her own name   doesn't know it at all
No she doesn't   she doesn't even know her own name

But yours she knows   O yours she knows –
You pimp-fucker – she knows yours
                very well

Of the Justice of the Liver & the Guts

this is poetry ground
from seven cranes of herakles
gantries are hanging suspended
roofs toppled off backwards
from seven corners of the homeland
we are the people
shoulder to shoulder   aaah!
with our forearms
ferrying our fists at the sky
with the demolished house beneath our marching feet
there is the smell of fennel & tikhum
any state worker & leased people
of all fabrics & any gender
made from construction plant industries
made by hand in factories
under our clenched jaws
it tastes of liver blood
in the justice of justice there to be taken
in the justice of words that from temple to toe are human
in the justice of seven that seven times beats in the chest of
                       the bullet & the heart fails
in the justice of the sun when in its absence
the town's little lights
are jezebel girls
in the justice of bread that without water can't get drown the throat
in the justice of a name that in my gulp has continuously repented
                       becoming my mother

in the justice of razors familiar with wrist blood
in the justice of darkness that – devoid of its presence – lovers are
                                        wasted
in the justice of salt that sucked up Urmia's sea in one gulp & so
        Urmia of Zartosht was ravelled in a flood of salt & cloth
in the justice of the liver's blood & guts
if if if I were to open my mouth
like Golestan's forests you'd be ablaze
I will bite into your raw liver so hard
the walls of Evin & Qezel Hesar & Gohardasht will become
                                        crow-flight
in the dreams of torturers wild pigs & hogs careen backwards
& revolution revolution will gush from your seven corners
& your seven ancestors & orifices will become a gobbling table
& the largest bone of my poem
                        will stick in your throat
so pieces of this blood land & body land & poetry land
will red-yelping-hood-it out from your eyeballs &
                        your larynx.

13

در خوابهای کاهویی که عشق انار انار بوته است

بهوقت لبها و چاکهام سرخ و چاک چاک از بوسه آخ

مرا باید تو را.... که باید

بهوقت بریدگی صدا زبان نفس بریدگی

در اوج اوج لذت زنی تن زندگی

در جدال با مَردُم مَرد مُردگی

مرا باید تو را.... که باید

در این هوای مَلس که سخت میچسبد باصفا

به سقف سقّ سیاهم بیا میآیمت

مرا باید تو را... که باید

با حالتهای صمیمیی تنها که تَکبهتَک به نُت میآیند

تُکبهتُک با سوءِتفاهمها که سوی تفاهم دارند

بهوقت انگشت روی پلکهام آتش مالیدن

نوشیدنِ خفیفِ خواب از پشت گوشهام اژدهام

مرا باید تو را... که باید ریختن شَک شُک شقِ حنجره

بیدار باش

باش

که باید تو را... باید مرا که باید

Collage Poem 13

From its green slumber   love splits pomegranate's red seeds
From the time of all my lips   red & slit-open from kissing & sighing
Aah!

It has to be for me…   For me you have to be…
                    I have to let you   see…

To the time of being slit open   voice language breath-death
At the high height of joy   woman-nexus   woman core spirit
In the great fight for people   male-sever   man death-perate

It has to be for me…   For me you have to be…

In the meltdown of milky air   such gold my dear dervish
To the soot-roof of my mouth   come   so I will come
It has to be for me…   For me you have to be…

With the song-shine between two close bodies   one by one peeling
                              to their shrieking
Cheek by jewel that through mistaking they'll come to understand
In the time of my fingers smudging fire onto my eyelids
And slip a sip of dream from just behind my ear   fire-dragon

It has to be for me…   For me you have to be   without suspicion
                              shockless
                         with vocal chords
                              erect

To wake up being   I have to let you see
That has to be you…   has to be me   has to be

I Have Poured Myself to the Wind

A curl of the eyelash a furl of the lips and with two bitter almonds
      in your face your face scarred to the bone by a brand
If you cut into my skin you will know what I'm saying There's a
      line through this writing looks like it's burnt

Truth or lies I don't know I only know you & this that whenever I'm
returning from you my hand becomes frozen and I walk zig-zaggedly
exactly like now when the pen doesn't fit well in my hand and the word
like a thread winds about the feet of my lines & your eye's almond flips
      over onto my skirt and stares out at me from there bitterly

There is no way back, I have decanted myself to the winds up to my waist
and nothing in anything of me can be put back for you again
And the world is a severed bridge that cannot carry anyone across to
anyone any longer and from all the corners of a few houses just a few
pillars without cornice or plinth remain swaying in mid-air I am the
explorer of the breath that I have plummeted down I have fallen in
      love with breathlessness & of a sudden in this air-deprived
      atmosphere I have become the breather of all breath

And the sun and the snow mountains and the bullfinch that flies from
that branch of the tree where we once lay and everything moves from
anywhere & everything flies from any place & everyone from anywhere
dead or alive, all all all of them breathe from inside me even love when
      it becomes short of breath takes its needy gasps from me

Where are you going from me where am I gone what does this mean?

And when you shackle my feet and…
With shackled feet I have been dancing all the way and with those
shackled feet I have come dancing from the tops of unnamed graves and I
know the names of the dead ones   one by one and by heart like
      my pearl drops of rain

Where, where can you wrap rope, chains, roads around my voice-breath?

"Say it" I said "Say it" Say my name and put its end-stop End it OK

Love's Lemony, as Lemon Is

If you take away this pink veil from my face
Love is the lemon colour that lemon-limps its
 way to the tangerine sun

Eyelashes and neck
Eyelashes cockeyed and neck skew-whiffed
Crooked into your shoulder-nooks
That seem like children's doodle-drawn homes
My head is craned down to your cranny bone
We are stood two crazed souls in each other
Stood neck to neck
Shoulder to shudder

Eyelashes and neck just there
Craned round again in the whorl of hot bone
And your eyes that kissing-kissed wet my lips
And your eyes that wet the kisses of my other lip
Your eye that plunges its furrow until we can't see
Fused in the voice and rapture of it

Come, come if you take the pink slowly from here
Love is lemony, as lemon is, and limps lemon-bitter
 then leaps to the tangerine womb

Lesgi / Dance

Lesgi that blade shudders grenade pins
lesgi that shatter stomps grapes into wine
that cuts the deck of earth & explodes love
that fountains the dream into its language
– language that tricks out its own dream –
and the fall & rise of throat breath, lesgi
on the top & back of the air flares, lesgi
inside clerical weapons & criminal sham
inside chemical weapons & crimson blood
lesgi .. gi .. go grow to the height of breath
heave the devil's tail up its own backside
head-butt your head on death's forehead
rub your shoulders on the cold air, lesgi
pure heart matter pulsing and pumping
stamp a one-step-forward two-back dance
sit dance sleep softer than soil-fallen rain
hailstones & wolverines kneeing into stone
slapping pain on calm's tender balm, lesgi
a girl's eye on the frontline cobraing right
a young guy sleeving away hidden poisons
bitterness on the rim and lining of the cup
there at the roundtable of bluebirds, lesgi
with listening devices there in all corners
with camera babes sat round their tables
with king & clown & killer, lesgi
– you're deer & tiger & forest – lesgi
– you leap on sabre & broken glass – lesgi
ever straining one neck higher than before
sufi of all dancers, my young sufis – lesgi
there at the height of the minaret – lesgi
the swung censer of the high altar – lesgi
circling spun dancer between sun & time,
& poem-breath from Shams' azure roots,
lesgi – from life to life dance, lesgi, dance,
live & don't die, lesgi, don't ever die

Katherine M. Hedeen

Afterword:
How to Create a Global Positioning System with the Highest Level of Errancy

(after *Hopscotch,* after Sidney West)

Employ the following coordinates.

Follow the map.

countercoordinate -37.4798549° southnorth
(page such and such verse whichever)

What is the point of my reaching her?
What is the point of my having reached her?

An arrow is a line between two points that directs somewhere

      we produce a vertex
      a vertex of ice

when released, the arrow points to the earth

countercoordinate 900000.68422° east
(page such and such verse whichever)

in the justice of the liver's blood & guts
if if if I were to open my mouth

telephone: listen

                    if it (rings)

                            it rings and why not

               isolate ambient noise
          because of (your ears)

countercoordinate 1.1111111° westwest
(page such and such verse whichever)

Night passes near you like some deaf beast
(it has nothing to do with the night
that the singers praise).
It passes near
but does not see you.

And at night twist the knife
skip into the garden
abandon all this,
it reeks of death.

The wood is dark enough by itself
Twist and turn, turn and twist –
Patient friction will bring on light
Before dawn

countercoordinate 5∞° south
(page such and such verse whichever)

amber silences

                accented oversights

breasts in flight from the mist

beneath fingernails

                  loyal urine

stains of inspiration

Like the way your throat is parched from thirst,

your body's birds combust – you must

Puffs of smoke leak from your lips

and birds that want to perch on my body become hot hot hotter by the day

Under a cascade of blood

        A hurling downpour

Who will be that fearless again

To risk

on another rooftop,

on another kilim,

Yet another game?

**countercoordinate √72.59876° north
(page such and such verse whichever)**

Which thread is the one that tells our story

and lends us substance

when there's no trajectory
by which to make sense of ourselves?
Which thread are we sure is vital?

you rise

in the allthetime collapsing back

you rise

in the allthetime cool

you rise

in the allthetime vibrating

you rise

in the allthetime expanding

you rise

in the allthetime nothing

you rise

in the allthetime collapsing angel-me

Whose ~~woods~~ words are these?

Acknowledgements

Najwan Darwish, translated by Kareem James Abu-Zeid, "A House in Kadiköy", "A Woman from the Other Side", "Out of This Cellar", "When I Saw Time", "While Sleeping in His New Home", "A Thought Occurs", "Like Everyone Else", "The Day Leaves You", "It Never Happened Before", "I Didn't Know", "On Half a Wing", "Happiness, in Three Parts", from *Kadiköy*. Reproduced with the permission of the author and translator.

Kim Hyesoon, translated by Don Mee Choi, "Pig Pigs Out" and "Bloom, Pig!"from I'm *OK, I'm Pig!* (Bloodaxe, 2014) © Don Mee Choi 2014. Reproduced with the permission of the author, the translator and Bloodaxe Books. "IS THERE WHITE LIGHT FOR US?," "Bird's Repetition," and "Glimmer — You Must," copyright © 2022 by Kim Hyseoon, translation copyright © 2022 by Don Mee Choi. Forthcoming from New Directions in the collection *Phantom Pain Wings* in 2023. Reprinted by permission of New Directions Publishing Corp.

Maria Stepanova, translated by Sasha Dugdale, "If Air" from *Старый мир. Починка жизни* (Новое издательство – Novoye izdatel'stvo, 2020). Reproduced with the permission of the author and translator.

Ana María Rodas, translated by Dan Eltringham, "Sunday 12 September, 1937", "Made of memories", "Strike a virgin pose", "Let us wash our hair", "You cleaned off the cum", "Sure", "They said a poem", "New lover", "You do well, great maestro", "Perhaps I'll leave the struggle", "I know", "Revolutionary", from *Poemas de la izquierda erótica* (Testimonio del Absurdo Diario, 1973). Reproduced with the permission of the author and translator. The Spanish text of "Domingo 12 de septiembre" is reprinted here with permission of papelesmínimos.

Coral Bracho, translated by Forrest Gander, "(Alzheimer's. Follow-up)", "(Diary) You're a bunch of thieves", "(Intuitions) Meaning is what accommodates things", "(Intuitions) The last thing that holds you up", "(Intuitions) Which thread is the one", "(Observations) That bird…", "(Observations) The puzzle pieces…", "(She speaks) I don't want that woman ever / to come back", "And let's see the red face of a jaguar that turns into a cat"; all from *It Must Be a Misunderstanding*, copyright ©2021, 2022 by Coral Bracho. Copyright © 2021, 2022 by Forrest Gander. Reprinted by permission of New Directions Publishing Corp.

Eva Kristina Olsson, translated by Johannes Göransson, excerpt from *The Angelgreen Sacrament* (Black Square Editions, 2021). Reproduced with the permission of the author and translator.

Víctor Rodríguez Núñez, translated by Katherine M. Hedeen, excerpt from *El cuaderno de la rata almizclera / the muskrat notebook* (Buenos Aires Poetry 2017). Reproduced with the permission of the author and translator.

Meena Kandasamy, translations of poems by Thiruvalluvar, "Berating Her Heart" and "The Delights of Sulking" from *The Book of Desire* by Meena Kandasamy (Galley Beggar Press, 2023). Reproduced with the permission of Galley Beggar Press and the translator.

Mehdi Akhavan Saless, translated by Ghazal Mosadeq, excerpt from *Then, After Thunder*. Reproduced with the permission of the Estate of Mehdi Akhavan Saless and the translator.

Chus Pato, translated by Erín Moure, "There are images that…", "Self-Portrait or Encounter with Gesture and Ancient Psyche", "Ethos" and "stalker", are all from *Sonora*, manuscript in progress. Reproduced with the permission of the author and translator.

Frédéric Forte, translated by Zoë Skoulding, "Moitié Oiseau", "Halfbird", "Reveille", "Offend Maggie" and "Break-up Song" from *Dire Ouf* (P.O.L. 2016). Reproduced with permission of the author, translator and P.O.L.

Ziba Karbassi, translated by Stephen Watts, "Breath: The Elixir Of Poetry", "Diwan Under Snow", "Sigh Poem 77", "Sigh Poem 78", "Sigh Poem 79", "Resistance", "Of The Justice Of The Liver & The Guts", "Collage Poem 13" "I Have Poured Myself to the Wind", "Love's Lemony, as Lemon Is", "Lesgi / Dance". Reproduced with the permission of the author and translator.

Zoë Skoulding would like to acknowledge support from the UK Arts and Humanities Research Council [grant number AH/T007087/1].

Contributors

Kareem James Abu-Zeid, PhD, is a translator of poets and novelists from across the Arab world who translates from Arabic, French, and German. His work has earned him an NEA translation grant, PEN Center USA's Translation Award, *Poetry* magazine's translation prize, residencies from the Lannan Foundation and the Banff Centre, a Fulbright Fellowship (Germany), and a CASA Fellowship (Egypt), among other honors. His most recent translation is Najwan Darwish's *Exhausted on the Cross* (NYRB Poets, 2021). He is also the author of *The Poetics of Adonis and Yves Bonnefoy: Poetry as Spiritual Practice*. The online hub for his work is www.kareemjamesabuzeid.com.

Mehdi Akhavan Saless was a leading Modernist poet of Iran. He was born in 1928 in Mashhad, and died in Tehran in 1990. He published under the pseudonym M. Omid. His major artistic preoccupation was the Iranian coup of 1953, after which he was imprisoned twice.

Mexican poet and translator **Coral Bracho** was born in Mexico City, where she still lives and teaches. She is the author of several collections of poetry, including *Ese espacio, ese jardín* (2003) which won the Xavier Villaurrutia Prize. Her poetry was translated for the Poetry Translation Center's 2005 World Poets' Tour by Tom Boll and poet Katherine Pierpoint. Bracho's honors include the Aguascalientes National Poetry Prize and a Guggenheim Fellowship. Her latest work in translation by Forrest Gander is *It Must be a Misunderstanding* published in 2022 by New Directions in the USA and Carcanet in the UK.

Born in Seoul, South Korea, **Don Mee Choi** is the author of the National Book Award winning collection *DMZ Colony* (Wave Books, 2020), *Hardly War* (Wave Books, 2016), *The Morning News Is Exciting* (Action Books, 2010), and several pamphlets of poems and essays, including *Translation is a Mode=Translation is an Anti-Neocolonial Mode* (Ugly Duckling Presse, 2020). She is a recipient of the 2021 MacArthur Fellowship and Guggenheim Fellowship.

Najwan Darwish (b. 1978) is one of the foremost contemporary Arab poets. Since the publication of his first collection in 2000, his poetry has been hailed across the Arab world and beyond as a singular expression of the Palestinian struggle. He has published eight books in Arabic, and his work has been translated into more than twenty languages. NYRB Poets published Darwish's *Nothing More to Lose,* translated by Kareem James Abu-Zeid, in 2014, which was picked as one of the best books of the year by NPR and nominated for several awards. His second major collection in English, *Exhausted on the Cross,* was published by NYRB Poets in 2021, with a Foreword by Raúl Zurita. Darwish lives between Haifa and his birthplace, Jerusalem.

Sasha Dugdale is a poet, translator and former editor of the magazine *Modern Poetry in Translation*. She is a Fellow of the Royal Society of Literature and writer-in-residence at St John's College, Cambridge. She has published many translations of Russian poetry. *Birdsong on the Seabed* (Bloodaxe) by Elena Shvarts, was a Poetry Book Society Choice and shortlisted for the Popescu and Academica Rossica Translation Awards. *War of the Beasts and the Animals* (Bloodaxe) by Maria Stepanova won a PEN Translates Award and was a Poetry Book Society Choice. Her translation of *In Memory of Memory*, a prose work by Maria Stepanova (Fitzcarraldo Editions), was shortlisted for the International Booker Prize, the James Tait Black Prize and was longlisted for the National Book Awards in the USA and the Baillie Gifford Prize. She has published five collections of poetry with Carcanet. Her monologue-poem 'Joy' won the 2016 Forward Prize for Best Single Poem, and her fifth collection *Deformations* was shortlisted for the T. S. Eliot and Derek Walcott Prizes. *Deformations* was an Observer Book of the Year.

Daniel Eltringham is a scholar, poet and translator based between Bristol and Sheffield, currently working on a comparative research project, *Translating Resistance*. His monograph, *Poetry & Commons: Postwar and Romantic Lyric in Times of Enclosure*, is out with Liverpool University Press (2022). Recent poetry and (co)translations have appeared in a range of magazines: *Firmament, Ludd Gang, Revista Kokoro, Protean* and *Cambridge Literary Review*, as well as in the anthology of poetry in translation, *Temporary Archives* (Arc, 2022). A chapbook of his translation of Alonso Quesada's *Scattered Ways* was published by Free Poetry (Boise, 2019) and his poetry collection *Cairn Almanac* was published by Hesterglock Press (Bristol, 2017). With Leire Barrera-Medrano he co-edits Girasol Press, a small publisher that explores handmade poetics and experimental translation.

Frédéric Forte was born in Toulouse, France, in 1973, and lives in Paris. He has been a member of the well-known Oulipo (Workshop of Potential Literature) since 2005 and runs the MFA in Creative writing in Le Havre. He has published 12 collections of poetry, including *Dire ouf* (P.O.L, Paris, 2016); more recently *Nous allons perdre deux minutes de lumière* (P.O.L, 2021) and *De la pratique* (l'Attente, Bordeaux, 2022), and several chapbooks. Three of his books have been translated into English: *Seven String Quartets* (La Presse/Fence Books, Iowa City, 2014; translation by Matthew B. Smith), *Minute-Operas* (Burning Deck, Providence, 2015; translation by Daniel

Levin Becker, Ian Monk, Michelle Noteboom and Jean-Jacques Poucel) and *33 Flat Sonnets* (Mindmade Books, Los Angeles, 2016; translation by Emma Ramadan). He has also translated into French the American poets Michelle Noteboom and Guy Bennett.

Forrest Gander, a writer and translator with degrees in geology and literature, was born in the Mojave Desert and lives in northern California. His books, often concerned with ecology, include *Twice Alive* and *Be With*, winner of the Pulitzer Prize. Gander's translations include *Alice Iris Red Horse*: Poems by Gozo Yoshimasu and *Then Come Back: the Lost Neruda Poems*. His newest titles are *Knot*, a collaboration with photographer Jack Shear, and *Names & Rivers* by Shuri Kido, translated with Tomoyuki Endo. His latest translation of Coral Bracho, *It Must be a Misunderstanding*, published by Carcanet in 2022, also includes the earlier work *Firefly Under the Tongue*.

Johannes Göransson (1973) is the author of several books of poetry, prose and criticism, including *Transgressive Circulation: Essays on Translation* and *Summer*, a book of poems. He is also the translator of books by several poets, including Aase Berg, Ann Jäderlund, Helena Boberg and Eva Kristina Olsson. He is one of the editors of Action Books and teaches at the University of Notre Dame.

Katherine M. Hedeen is a translator and essayist. A specialist in Latin American poetry, she has translated some of the most respected voices from the region. Her publications include book-length collections by Jorgenrique Adoum, Juan Bañuelos, Juan Calzadilla, Antonio Gamoneda, Fina García Marruz, Juan Gelman, Fayad Jamís, Raúl Gómez Jattin, Hugo Mujica, José Emilio Pacheco, and Víctor Rodríguez Núñez, among many others. Her work has been a finalist for both the Best Translated Book Award and the National Translation Award. She is a recipient of two NEA Translation Grants in the US and a PEN Translates award in the UK. She is a Managing Editor for Action Books. She resides in Ohio, where she is Professor of Spanish at Kenyon College. More information at: www.katherinemhedeen.com

Kim Hyesoon is one of the most influential contemporary poets of South Korea. Her most recent poetry in translation, *Autobiography of Death* (New Directions, 2018), won the 2019 International Griffin Poetry Prize. She has received numerous prestigious literary awards, including the 2022 Samsung Ho-Am Prize. Her new collection, *Phantom Pain Wings*, is forthcoming from New Directions. Her earlier volumes of poetry in translation can be found at actionbooks.org.

Meena Kandasamy is a poet, writer, translator, anti-caste activist and academic. Her extensive corpus includes two poetry collections, *Touch* (2006) and *Ms Militancy* (2010), as well as three novels, *The Gypsy Goddess* (2014), *When I Hit You* (2017) and *Exquisite Cadavers* (2019). Her translation of Salma's *Manamiyangal* (Women Dreaming, 2020) won a PEN Translates Award. Her feminist translation of the Kamathuppaal (*The Book of Desire*) from the Thirukkural is forthcoming from Galley Beggars Press in 2023. Working with the National Centre for Writing, Norwich, she has mentored several emerging literary translators in the last couple of years.

Ziba Karbassi was born in Tabriz, north-western Iran & fled her country as a young teenager in the mid 1980s, since when she has lived mostly in London. She has published ten books of poetry in Persian, the chapbook *Collage Poems* (Exiled Writers Ink 2009) in English translation and *Poesie* (MilleGru 2011) in Italian. She is widely regarded as one of the most accomplished Persian poets of her generation. Her poems have appeared in many journals throughout Europe & US, including *Poetry Review* and *Modern Poetry in Translation*, and are included in various anthologies, most recently *Essential Voices : Poetry of Iran & Its Diaspora* (Iowa: Green Linden Press, 2021). She also gives frequent, vivid performances of her work, and has read widely, from the Southbank's National Poetry Library to San Francisco. She was chairperson of the Iranian Writers Association (in exile) from 2002 to 2004, editor of *Asarnameh* & on the editorial committee of *Exiled Ink* magazine in London (acting also as Chair of Exiled Writers Ink between 2012 & 2014). In 2010 she won the Golden Apple Poetry Prize for Azerbaijan & in 2012 she was chosen by the Contemporary Poetics Research Centre (CPRC) at Birkbeck College, University of London, as a 'revolutionary world poet'. A book of her work in English translation (co-translated with Stephen Watts) awaits publication.

Ghazal Mosadeq is a poet, editor and translator. She is the founder of Pamenar Press, an independent press with an interest in plurilingual and multicultural experimental poetry and translation, and is a member of the editorial advisory board for the *Journal of British and Irish Innovative Poetry*. Her poetry and critical writing have been published in Iran by Morvarid, Negah and Hirmand, and in the UK by gammm Press (in English and Italian), Tamaas Foundation, Litmus Press, *Poetry Wales*, *Teflon* (Greek), *WD40*, *Revista de poesía, ensayo y crítica* (Spanish), *Senna Hoy* (French and English), *Oversound* and *Blackbox Manifold* among others.

Erín Moure is a poet and translator with 18 books of poetry, a co-authored book of poetry, a volume of essays, a book of articles on translation, a poetics, and two memoirs; she has translated or co-translated 21 books of poetry and two of biopoetics from French, Spanish, Galician, Portuguese, and Ukrainian, by poets such as Nicole Brossard (with Robert Majzels), Andrés Ajens, Chantal Neveu, Rosalía de Castro, Chus Pato, Uxío Novoneyra, Lupe Gómez (with Rebeca Lema Martínez and on her own), Fernando Pessoa, and Yuri Izdryk (with Roman Ivashkiv). Three of her own books have appeared in translation, one each in German, Galician, and French. Her work has received the Governor General's Award twice, Pat Lowther Memorial Award, A. M. Klein Prize twice, and has been a three-time finalist for the Griffin Prize and three-time finalist in the USA for a Best Translated Book Award (Poetry). Her latest is *The Elements* (2019) and *Theophylline: an a-po'etic migration* will appear in 2023.

Eva Kristina Olsson (1958) is the author of several books of poetry and plays, as well as a dancer, performer and filmmaker. She has published many books – including *The Crime* (1988), *Eiderwhite* (2011), and the verse plays *Antigone's Face Niobe's Labyrinth* (2013). The English translation of her book *The Angelgreen Sacrament* was published in 2021 (Black Square Editions).

Chus Pato (Ourense, 1955) writes in Galician and is the author of 11 books of poems, published between 1991 and 2019. Several books of hers have been translated and published in the USA, UK, Canada, Spain, Argentina, Portugal, Netherlands, and Bulgaria, and her poems have been included in dozens of Galician, Spanish, and international anthologies. She is a member of PEN Galicia and the Royal Galician Academy. She has performed at poetry festivals throughout Europe and the Americas, and her work has received various prizes including the Spanish National Critics' Prize and, twice, the Losada Diéguez Prize. Pato lives in central Galicia in NW Spain, close to the Catasós forest, home to the oldest chestnut trees in Europe. Her most recent book is *Un libre favor*, translated into English by Erín Moure as *The Face of the Quartzes* (Veliz Books, 2021).

Ana María Rodas was born in 1937 in Guatemala City, where she lives. A Guatemalan poet, journalist, and teacher, she has published around twenty books since announcing her arrival on the literary scene in 1973 with *Poemas de la izquierda erótica*. One of the leading figures of Guatemalan and Central American feminism, her work has been translated into English, German, Portuguese and Italian. In 1990, she simultaneously won the poetry and short story categories of the Juegos Florales de México, Centroamérica y el Caribe. In 2000, she won the prestigious Miguel Ángel Asturias National Prize in Literature for her life's work. In 2017, she received the honour of being recognized as an Illustrious Person for her contribution to universal literature by San Carlos University of Guatemala on its three-hundredth anniversary, and in 2018 she was made an honorary member of the Guatemalan Centre of PEN International.

Víctor Rodríguez Núñez (Havana, 1955) is one of Cuba's most outstanding and celebrated contemporary writers, with over seventy collections of his poetry published throughout the world. He has been the recipient of major awards in the Spanish-speaking region, including, in 2015, the coveted Loewe Prize and most recently the Manuel Alcántara Prize. His selected poems have been translated into Arabic, Chinese, English, French, German, Hebrew, Italian, Macedonian, Serbian, Swedish, and Vietnamese and he has read his poetry in more than fifty countries. In the last decade, his work has developed an enthusiastic readership in the US and the UK, where he has published seven book-length translations. He divides his time between Gambier, Ohio, where he is currently Professor of Spanish at Kenyon College, and Havana, Cuba. More information at: www.victorrodrigueznunez.com

Zoë Skoulding's most recent collections of poetry are *A Marginal Sea* (Carcanet, 2022) and *A Revolutionary Calendar* (Shearsman Books, 2020). Her previous collections (published by Seren Books) include *The Mirror Trade* (2004); *Remains of a Future City* (2008), shortlisted for Wales Book of the Year; *The Museum of Disappearing Sounds* (2013), shortlisted for the Ted Hughes Award for New Work in Poetry; and *Footnotes to Water* (2019), which was a Poetry Book Society Recommendation and won the Wales Book of the Year Poetry Award 2020. She received the Cholmondeley Award in 2018. Her poetry has been translated into over 30 languages, and is included in *Nuestra tierra de nadie. Antología de la poesía galesa contemporánea*, (México: La Otra Ediciones, 2015 / Bogotá: Ladrones del Tiempo, 2018), translated and edited by Víctor Rodríguez Núñez and Katherine M. Hedeen. She is the translator (from French) of Jean Portante's *In Reality: Selected Poems* (Seren, 2013). Her work as a critic includes *Contemporary Women's Poetry and Urban Space: Experimental Cities* (Palgrave Macmillan, 2013), and *Poetry & Listening: The Noise of Lyric* (Liverpool University Press, 2020). She lives in Wales on Ynys Môn and is Professor of Poetry and Creative Writing at Bangor University.

Maria Stepanova is a poet, essayist, and journalist. Born in 1972, she graduated from Moscow Literary Institute in 1995. She is the author of ten poetry collections and three books of essays, and a recipient of several Russian and international literary awards, including the prestigious Andrey Bely Prize and Joseph Brodsky Foundation Fellowship. Her poems have been translated into many languages, including English, Italian, German, French, and Hebrew. She took part in a number of Russian and international literary festivals and programs focusing on modern poetry. Her documentary novel *Pamiati*

pamiati (In Memory of Memory) that blends memoir, documents, and essays into an epic narrative, came out in Russian in November 2017 and received the Big Book Prize in December 2018 and NOS prize in February 2019. The book was translated into numerous languages, shortlisted for the Booker Prize International and longlisted for the National Book Award.

Thiruvalluvar was a Tamil poet and philosopher thought to have written *Thirukkural* between 31 BCE and 400 CE. No reliable biographical details survive.

Stephen Watts is a poet, translator & research advocate/activist who has lived & worked in the richly multilingual Whitechapel communities of East London for near on 45 years. His most recent books include *Ancient Sunlight* (Enitharmon, 2014; repr. 2020) & *Republic of Dogs/Republic of Birds* (Test Centre 2016; 2nd edition, Prototype 2020). A b/w 16mm 70 minute film *The Republics* was made from the latter by Huw Wahl. Prototype published the first volume of Stephen's collected poems, *Journeys Across Breath: Poems 1975–2005*, in 2022 & *A Book of Drawn Poems* is also due from Joe Hales's Sylvia imprint in late 2022. Recent co-translations include *Pages from the Biography of an Exile* by Adnan al-Sayegh (Arc Publications, 2014) & Golan Haji's *A Tree Whose Name I Don't Know* (New York: A Midsummer Night's Press, 2017). A book by the Iranian poet Ziba Karbassi awaits publication & co-translations of two other Iranian writers, Esmail Khoi & Reza Baraheni, are also forthcoming. His translation research was the subject of two recent exhibitions: 'Swirl of Words/ Swirl of Worlds' at PEER Gallery, Hoxton, for which he edited a book of that title & subtitled *Poems from 94 Languages Spoken Across Hackney* & 'Explosion of Words' (which celebrated his 2,000 page *Bibliography of Modern Poetry in English Translation*) at the Sträuhof Gallery, Zurich & Nunnery Gallery, Bow, in summer 2021 & in 2022 respectively. His own poetry is translated into many languages, with books in Italian, Czech, Arabic, German & Spanish.

Ingram Content Group UK Ltd.
Milton Keynes UK
UKHW010906170323
418668UK00001B/1

9 781848 618510